Charles Edward Turner

The Modern Novelists of Russia

Being the substance of six lectures delivered at the Taylor Institution, Oxford

Charles Edward Turner

The Modern Novelists of Russia
Being the substance of six lectures delivered at the Taylor Institution, Oxford

ISBN/EAN: 9783337028510

Printed in Europe, USA, Canada, Australia, Japan

Cover: Foto ©Thomas Meinert / pixelio.de

More available books at **www.hansebooks.com**

THE

MODERN NOVELISTS

OF

RUSSIA

*BEING THE SUBSTANCE OF SIX LECTURES
DELIVERED AT THE TAYLOR INSTITUTION, OXFORD*

BY

CHARLES EDWARD TURNER

ENGLISH LECTOR IN THE UNIVERSITY OF ST. PETERSBURG

LONDON

TRÜBNER & CO., LUDGATE HILL

1890

THE MODERN NOVELISTS OF RUSSIA.

LECTURE I.

IVAN ALEXANDROVITCH GONCHAROFF.

THE Russian novel did not easily, or till within a comparatively recent period, obtain its right of citizenship in the world of letters. The purists of the eighteenth century were ill-disposed to allow the claim of the novelist to rank with the dramatist or poet; whilst the Church sharply denounced romances as injurious and prejudicial to public morality. "From the reading of novels," writes Sumarokoff, the great literary authority of those days, and the founder of the modern Russian theatre, "we can get little good and risk getting much harm. We have no right to call it an amusement, it is rather a hurtful waste of time." An anonymous pamphleteer of the same period, whose fierceness of style perhaps justifies us in supposing him to have been an ecclesiastic, condemns romances as being " the

B

deadliest of all the weapons employed by the
devil against the soul of man." If we turn to the
novels themselves, we find them to be irredeem-
ably dull, and their extremely limited number,
seldom more than two or three a year being published in the whole of Russia, would betoken an
indifference on the part of the public that makes
it difficult to understand how they ever could have
provoked such bitter hostility. When not direct
translations from the French, they were closely
modelled on Fénélon or Scarron, and accordingly
were either sermons in the form of fiction, as
edifying as they were tedious, or else portrayals
of a life that had nothing in common with the
habits and traditions of the Russian people.

As the earlier stages of Russian civilisation are
marked by the bitter struggle of two opposing
parties for pre-eminence, the one desirous to impress a new and foreign-exported social code upon
the people, the other zealous to preserve, as far as
possible, untouched the national life and traditions
of the past; so, in the history of Russian literature
we observe, from its very commencement, two like
conflicting elements. In spite of his heavy, monotonous, unformed style, Kantemier, the first in
point of date of Russian poets, has given us in his
nine satires a faithful picture of the manners and

belief of his times, and it is in their nationality that their true, it may be their only, value resides. Even when imitating the satires of Horace, Juvenal, or Boileau, he never fails to accommodate these imitations to the necessities of Russian life. The vices he exposes are not the vices of a past or foreign civilisation, but those which stained the society of his own age and country. He chiefly attacks those of his countrymen who, unable to comprehend the full significance and bearing of the reforms inaugurated by Peter, and still further carried out by Catherine, idly imagined that they were aiding the cause of progress by aping foreign customs, copying the fashions of Western Europe, and heartily despising everything Russian. Unfortunately, his rude diction and still ruder versification did not allow Kantemier to become a model for the writers who followed him, and the place of literary lawgiver was reserved for his more illustrious contemporary, Lomonosoff, who exchanged the dull syllabic metre hitherto exclusively employed for a richer and more varied form of verse, and who gave a new life to the Russian language by freeing it from archaic barbarisms and endowing it with a constructive polish and grace it had never known before. Seeing that his predecessors taught him nothing except what

he had better avoid, and unable to find in them
any sure foundation whereon to build, it is only
natural that Lomonosoff should have gone to
foreign sources for his inspiration.   Consequently,
his poems are little more than transcripts of French
or German thought and expression, are marked by
a complete absence of originality, abound with
stereotyped pseudo - classical figures of speech,
which, from constant repetition, had lost whatever
meaning they once possessed, and are thoroughly
non-Russian in spirit and tone.

The persistency with which these classical affectations maintained their hold in Russian literature
is best to be seen in the works of those writers
who, following the example set by Kantemier,
tried to bring poetry and the novel into close and
direct union with the cares and hopes of the
actual world around them.   We may select, by
way of example, Karamsin's once famous, now
almost forgotten, romance, "Poor Louisa."   It is
evidently modelled on Richardson's "Pamela,"
for which Karamsin always expressed the warmest
admiration, declaring its author to be "the most
artistic painter of man's moral nature."   But though
it pretends to be a story of humble life, the writer
carefully adheres to the literary traditions of his
age.   The poor peasant girl is made to talk and act

like a fine heroine, her conversation is couched in a style as far as possible removed from the language of ordinary people, and she perpetually indulges in high-flown gushing tirades which would scarcely be tolerated in the most sentimental of melo-dramas. Old modes of speech, that had long been banished from daily conversation, and were reserved solely for official documents, and bookish forms of words, supposed to have a solemnity which would be wanting to them if presented in their ordinary shape, are put into the mouths of pea-sants, who, in real life, would never think of employing them. But we must not blame the novelist for thus idealising his characters. In so doing he but satisfied the tastes of his epoch. Nor should we forget that exactly those portions of the tale which offend us as being unnatural and lachrymose, won from contemporary critics the warmest praise and loudest applause. It was a bold venture to select for his subject the fate of a common peasant family, but at least its members had to be washed, combed, and well dressed be-fore they could be judged worthy to excite the interest and gain the sympathy of polite and cultured readers.

What I have just said of Karamsin applies equally to his immediate successors, who, whilst

aiming to reflect in their romances the life of the
age in which they wrote, and, whilst acknowledging that the poet should be the interpreter,
not only of the loftier manifestations of humanity,
but also of the daily worries, trivialities, and solemn
nothings of man's existence, none the less considered it necessary to give an idyllic tone to their
works.   Their peasant characters are far too arca
dian to be true portraitures, whilst their nobles are
nothing more than copies of the heroes of French
romance, bearing Russian names and swaggering
about in Russian costumes.   Their highly-coloured
pictures of Russian country life remind us of
Manieloff, in Gogol's " Dead Souls," who, we are
told, "was by nature excessively sugary," indulged
in pleasant dreams as to what he meant to do for
his serfs, and spent whole days in drawing elaborate
plans of pretty ivy-covered cottages, which he intended to build for them.   But, in the meantime,
their condition remained unaltered and unimproved,
nor was it possible to find in the whole district peasants worse lodged, or sunk in deeper wretchedness
or misery, than those who lived on the estates of
the good and tender-hearted Manieloff.   In the
same way, these sentimental writers, with their
fancy pictures of happy serfs and beneficent masters, only contributed to the indefinite postpone-

ment of any amelioration in the life of the bond-
man, tranquillised the public conscience, blinded
men to the sin of trafficking in human flesh, and
exalted serfdom into a patriarchal institution,
necessary to the due organisation and well-being
of the state.   By his stern exposure of the unnatural barbarities that accompanied the reign of
serfage, Gogol once and for ever freed Russian
literature from all this Manielovistic cant.

It is impossible to overestimate the influence
exercised by Gogol on Russian literature.   He
introduced into it a new and all-powerful element, that of realism.   In his humour, in his
irony, in his language, in his ideas, in his pathos,
in his occasional outbursts of lyrical eloquence,
Gogol is thoroughly Russian.   His characters
betray their nationality, not by wearing a *saraphan*,
but in their every word, in their way of looking at
things, and in their every act and gesture.   There
is no reason why Karamsin's " Poor Louisa "
should not have been written by a Frenchman or
by a German, but we cannot by any freak of the
fancy imagine Gogol's tales or comedies to have
been composed by any other than a Russian poet.
The narrow stifling circle that had hitherto formed
the source of the novelist's inspiration was exchanged for a wider and healthier sphere ; the

legendary exploits of historical heroes no longer
constituted the favourite theme of romancists;
and the serf-owner was stripped of the stage robes
in which poets had been pleased to drape him.
For the first time, in the pages of Gogol, the life
of the suffering poor, photographed from actual
observation, was revealed with a power of truthfulness that effectually aroused his countrymen from
the lethargic complacency with which they had so
long ignored the evils necessarily attached to a
system that entrusted a privileged class with
unlimited and irresponsible authority over all in
their employ.   With such fidelity to human nature
are his different personages delineated, that we
instinctively recognise them as old acquaintances
whom we have come across more than once, to
whom we could without difficulty give their true
names, and whose foibles, when recalled to our
memories, we immediately associate with a certain
Ivan or Masha.   It is their kinship to ourselves,
the knowledge that they are no fantastic creations,
but real living beings, that enlists our interests in
the humblest and meanest among them, and
makes us sympathise with them in their little joys
and struggling toil.   There is no single phase of
Russian life that Gogol has not seized on and
depicted; nor do I know of any writer, unless it

be our English Dickens, in whose works we shall find so many portraits that have become to all of us familiar and household names.

The radical reform effected by Gogol in Russian literature was no less enduring than it was beneficial. We cannot mention a single later writer who has not followed in his steps, and in his own way and after his peculiar genius carried on the work he began. For we must not forget that, at the time when Gogol wrote, the peasant class was · separated by a rigid and impassable line of demarcation from the so-called higher orders of society, and novelists, who introduced into their works sketches of serf-life, naturally wrote under the influence of this idea. With marvellous power Gogol reproduces in its every minutest detail the outward form of peasant life, and exposes the misery and degradation to which the serf was subjected ; but at the same time he makes us feel, and would seem himself to consider, the peasant to be something beneath and different to ourselves. It were foolish to blame Gogol for not doing more. The first step in progress was made when the eyes of the Russian people were opened to a recognition of the ill that had for generations been festering unnoticed and uncared for in their very midst. It remained for the writers who immediately

followed him to inspire them with the sure conviction that the free development of the latent
forces of the nation was, then, only possible when
serfdom had been completely and finally abolished.
In proof that Gogol and his successors each did
their work well, I may mention that, when the
author of "Dead Souls" read to Poushkin the
opening chapters of his work, the poet was so
struck with the miseries of the Russian peasantry,
for the first time revealed in all their naked hide-
ousness, that he cried out: "God! how wretched
life in Russia is." Of a more practical nature
was the impression produced by his perusal of
Tourgenieff's "Stories from a Sportsman's Note-
book" on the late emperor, Alexander II., who
once confessed to the novelist that, "after having
read it, he never for a minute doubted the
necessity of securing, as quickly as possible, the
full emancipation of the serfs."

In one and the same year, 1847, within less
than six years after the appearance of the first
part of Gogol's "Dead Souls," and within twelve
months after Dostoevsky had written his "Poor
People," Hertzen gave to the world, under the
pseudonym of Iskander, his best romance, "Who
is to Blame?" Goncharoff published his first
novel, "A Common Story," Grigorovitch wrote his

touching tale, "The Village," and Tourgenieff
contributed to the pages of "The Contemporary"
the opening chapters of his "Stories from a Sportsman's Notebook." The mere enumeration of
these works carries back the mind to the bright
epoch when the hopes of Russia began to beat
high, the "golden days," as Stchedrin proudly
calls them, when a spirit of enthusiasm, mixed, it
is true, with much that strikes us as ludicrous and
bombastic, was spread abroad, and when her best
men were nerved with the belief that the old order
of things would ere long be transformed and
brought into harmony with the wants and requirements of a progressive age. The realisation of
these hopes could, of course, be only ensured by
making the work of reform a common work, the
necessity of which should be acknowledged by all,
and in which all should take their part. For this
purpose, it was not sufficient to evoke pity for the
serf as mere serf, but the as yet unlearned lesson
had to be taught that the *moujik* is a man, that
beneath his rough sheepskin there beats a human
heart, and that in spite of the filth, poverty, and
ignorance to which the greed and apathy of his
owners had condemned him, he is still endowed
with the higher and kindlier instincts of our nature
that require only to be cultured. And besides

this, the nation at large must be compelled to recognise the empty worthlessness of the idle selfish lives led by those, on whose behalf and for whose profit the enslavement of the serf had so long and so harshly been maintained. These are the two lessons taught by the writers I have just mentioned; and for this reason, apart from any attraction their novels may possess as works of art and stories of human passion and suffering, they have a higher worth in their historical bearing, as interpreting to us the first steps made in the social and political regeneration of modern Russia.

We have only to compare the impression produced on us by Gogol's story, "The Cloak," and that left on our minds by Dostoevsky's "Poor People," to understand the significance and extent of the change that had come over the tone and tendency of Russian thought in the short interval separating the publication of these two tales. We pity Akakia Akakievitch, the poor shy copying-clerk, who, convinced of the impossibility of patching any more his one overcoat, nerves himself to form an extravagant resolution, the execution of which must involve the patient labour of more than one long year. He determines to purchase a new thickly-wadded cloak, and accordingly begins to practise the strictest economy, his whole income amounting to exactly one sovereign a month. His thrifty habits have in the end their full reward. The cloak is bought : but he is not allowed long to enjoy the realisation of the one idea of his life. On awaking the next morning from a glorious dream, in which he saw nothing but Akakias, in every form and posture, and all clothed in the newest and brightest of cloaks, he discovered that his cloak had been stolen during the night. But the story excites only our pity, nor is there one of its readers who would wish to be Akakia Akakievitch. The barrenness of a life like his repels us, and this feeling is intensified by the one act of energy that interrupts the monotony of his existence ; for in nothing does the debasing insignificance of his aims and ideas stand forth more prominently than in this exceptional, but paltry, activity. Very different is our feeling to-wards Dayvouschkin, the hero of Dostoevsky's tale. The complete absence of self-seeking in his love for Barbara, the delicacy with which he tries to represent to her every act of kindly help he renders as a mere whim on his part involving no sacrifice, his ill-concealed fear lest she should obtain the slightest taint or suffer the most trifling inconvenience from those with whom, owing to her

poverty, she is obliged to live and associate : these
and twenty other traits of character he unconsciously reveals in his letters to her, win for him
our envying sympathy, and compel the most
cultured and fastidious among us to confess that,
with all our culture and refinement, there is something in Dayvouschkin's unaffected way of thinking and acting to which we have not attained, and
that the dark damp hole in which he lodged was
warmed and lighted up by the illuminating presence of the divine.   Akakia Akakievitch denied
himself much, but it was to procure his own ease
and comfort ; Dayvouschkin denied himself everything, but it was for others : and in this resides the
whole difference between the two.

How necessary it was men should be taught
that through generations of suffering and privation
the poor despised serfs have maintained unshaken
that faith in God and that obedience to the law of
love, which the so-called intelligent class of Russia
has all but lost, or at the best despise as supersti-
tious and old-fashioned, we may judge from the
godless indifference with which their owners
habitually neglected and violated the commonest
and most ordinary rights of human brotherhood.
Thus, in " The Village," Grigorovitch relates how,
to amuse his young wife, who had never seen a

peasant-wedding, the noble hero gets up a marriage for her entertainment, and orders a young orphan girl on his estate to marry the peasant, whose name first comes into his head. After the conclusion of the ceremony, the newly-joined pair come to pay their respects to their master and mistress. To the great astonishment of the lady, the bride looks sad, and her face bears signs of recent weeping. But she is easily quieted, when her lord assures her that with the common people it is a traditional custom for brides to weep during the first week after their marriage. The same cynical disregard for the happiness and interests of others, the same insolent neglect of all moral obligations in the pursuit of one's own selfish ease, and the same crass ignorance of the rights common to rich and poor alike, characterise Madame Zvierkoff in Tourgenieff's tale, " Hermolaus and the Miller's Wife." She complains bitterly of what she terms "the black and monstrous ingratitude" of poor Irene, who actually has the presumption to ask her employer's leave to marry the man to whom she has long been engaged, though "she knows that her mistress has not another chambermaid to take her place, and that it is a rule of the house not to have married servants." And when the weeping girl throws herself at the feet of her ladyship, and tearfully prays for the sanction without which no peasant could marry, she at once raises her up, and blandly assures her that "we should never demean our-selves so far as to forget what is due to human dignity."

It is the universal recognition of this "human dignity," about which Madame Zvierkoff prates so glibly, that forms the fundamental principle of the social creed of the novelists of this period. This idea, I need scarcely say, is expressed most directly in the novels of Dostoevsky and Count Tolstoi. They have, to use Dostoevsky's favourite expression, "brought us to the people," made their life and faith our example and rule, and taught us how it is in the people that we must seek the real strength and power of a nation. But though Goncharoff, in his three novels, "A Common Story," "Oblomoff," and "The Precipice," introduces us into another world, and rarely selects his personages from the peasant class, the lesson these stories teach by implication, rather than directly, is the same.

Alexander Adoueff, the hero of the first of Goncharoff's novels, is a type of the cultured Russian in the old sleepy days, when every day, yesterday, to-day, and to-morrow, the bureaucratic machine of

government worked orderly, regularly, without rest,
and the wheels of the machine moved round and
round, without a single break or pause, grinding
all down to one uniform level, and ruthlessly
crushing everything that stood in the way of its
dull, monotonous march.   The spoilt son of a
fond mother, he soon learned the easy lesson of
regarding all round him as creatures sent into the
world for the express object of rendering his life
easy and comfortable, beings, whose excuse for
existing at all, is to anticipate his every whim, and
to humour his every caprice.   "You are the only
master here," are the words with which his mother
liked to console him, whenever he complained of
any faint show of opposition ; whilst the nurse was
ever croning into his ears sweet prophesies that he
would go through the world in robes of gold, and
should never know sorrow.   What wonder if he
accepted the adulation showered on him as the
just acknowledgment of his high worth and
exceptional talents ?   He, accordingly, had no
sooner finished his University studies than he resolved to go up to St. Petersburg, where his uncle,
Peter Ivanovitch, occupied a high government
post, and through whose protection Alexander
hoped to see his rare merits quickly appreciated
and rewarded.   He felt that a glorious future

awaited him, and that he had a special call to
accomplish some great work in the world.   Like
all dreamers of his time, the very indefiniteness of
the work, the achievement of which was to bring
him immortal fame, invested it in his eyes with a
peculiar charm. He, of course, might have stayed
on his estate, made his own home happier, and
spread that happiness over the little circle within
which his power and influence, for good or evil,
could be felt.   But Adoueff soared above such
narrowing limits.   His activity needed a wider
sphere, and nothing less than humanity, the whole
human   race,   could   satisfy   his   all-embracing
schemes of philanthropy and reform.   There is no
occasion to follow his career step by step; it could
only end in disappointment and failure.   Experience taught him the primary law of life, "Do the
duty which lies nearest thee," drove him back from
the unreal kingdoms in which he had sought impossible conquests, and made him acknowledge
that the one place wherein he could be of use to
himself or others, was that same tiny home-world
he had, in his ignorance, despised, as being too
hampered and confined.

It is difficult, perhaps impossible, for one unac-
quainted with Russian life as it was in the days of
an Adoueff, to appreciate the art and skill with

which the novelist has drawn the portrait of his hero. The character is apt to strike one as exaggerated and overdrawn. His ignorance of the world he goes forth so confidently to conquer must appear unnatural, if we do not recollect the pernicious training to which he had been exposed. And what is still more difficult for us to understand, is the comparatively undisturbed placidity with which, when he has learned, so far as he ever could learn, what the world really is, he accepts his defeat in the battle of life. But, unfortunately, there is in reality nothing strange or exceptional in his fate. All who have studied modern Russia must have been struck with the fact that, not only the Adoueffs, men radically weak in will and character, but, with few exceptions, her most prominent men, either die early or bring their career of activity to a premature end. The explanation is to be found in the conditions of Russian life, which are altogether unfavourable to the full and free development of the intellectual force and energy of the nation. It requires no ordinary physical, and a still rarer mental vigour to keep true to the creed of one's youth, when the slighfest display of individualism is visited as a crime, and is looked upon as being out of gear with the elaborate machinery of a bureaucratic administration. We thus find the majority of Russians, after a short and fitful *Sturm und Drang* period, and whilst still in the prime of life, rejecting what they call the utopias of youth ; and in this term is too often included every high moral standard and every high practical aim. They learn after a little experience that it is safer and wiser to mind their own affairs, to restrict their activity to making their own fortune, and believe themselves, and are esteemed by others, to be very useful, respectable members of society, if only they refrain from writing or talking about politics,—of all occupations the least profitable in Russia. If of a cynical temperament, they will henceforth scoff at, and hold up to ridicule the ideas to which they so loudly and so enthusiastically asserted their adherence in earlier days. If endowed with a kindlier and more genial nature, they will pardon and excuse the extravagances of youthful opinion, but at the same time will preach the necessity of these vagaries being quickly replaced by a more practical, that is, a more selfish and narrower view of things. It was so with Adoueff. At the beginning of his career, it may be, he was inspired with generous sentiments, indulged in the widest-reaching schemes, and looked eagerly forward to the day when he should be able to carry out his lofty principles. But he

remained true to his creed only till he entered the
world, and then, in presence of the deadening
exigencies of official life, abandoned his dreams,
and ended with burning what he had once adored,
and adoring what he had once burned. Not without reason, the novelist has given to his work the
meaning title, " A Common Story."

In his critical study, published in 1874, under
the title of " Better Late than Never," long after
the hot controversies provoked by his second and
greatest novel, " Oblomoff," had come to an end,
Goncharoff declares that his three romances are a
faithful reproduction of the experiences of his own
life, the description of what he had seen with his
own eyes. " I have never been able to write of
anything that has not grown up and ripened within
me, that I have not myself seen, observed, and
experienced. I have, or rather had, my own field,
my own soil, just as I have my own country ; my
own natal air, friends, and enemies ; my own little
corner, wherein I have observed, felt, and thought ;
and I have written only what I have lived through,
what I have thought, felt, and loved, what I have
seen close to me, and what I have known,—in a
word, I have described my own life, and what
grew into it, and made itself a part of that life."

These words admirably illustrate the bent of

Goncharoff's genius. He depicts life as it exhibited
itself around him, such as he found it, and presents
it in the forms it had in the course of ages assumed,—forms that had long existed, but which,
in part, already belonged to the past, or were in
the process of dying out.   He sees all that is
around him, and, endowed to a far higher degree
than any of his contemporaries with the power of
generalisation, he has, in the person of Oblomoff,
created a type of the old Russian character, which,
for breadth of conception and accuracy in minute
filling-up, has no equal in the literature of his
country.   But, unlike Dostoevsky and Count
Tolstoi, he does not possess the prophetic instinct
of looking ahead, and his descriptions of the
actual lack the suggestiveness that gives a charm,
and at the same time a peculiar value, to their
pictures of the present.

As I have already remarked, only those who
have themselves been brought into contact with it
can form an idea of the dull, monotonous existence
which the old-fashioned Russian country gentry
had from time immemorial been accustomed to
lead, and which they continued to pursue up to
the momentous year of the emancipation of the
serfs.   How can an Englishman be brought to
believe that there is no exaggerated distortion of

the truth in Goncharoff's description of the daily
home-life of the Oblomoffs, who, like the rest of
their class, slept away their existence, took no part
in the interests of the outer world, and were dead
to all the higher aims and nobler instincts of
humanity !   From an early hour in the morning
the noise of knives, as the cook and his underlings
in the kitchen chopped up the meat and the greens
for the soup, could be heard as far as the village ;
whilst from time to time the shrill whining tone of
the housekeeper's voice rose above the din, as she
gave her different orders and instructions.   In the
meantime, the master of the house was busily
engaged in sitting at the window of his room,
watching with untired energy all that went on in
the courtyard. "Hey, Ignasha, you blockhead,
what are you carrying there ? " he shouts to a serf
who then happened to pass by.   "I am taking the
knives to be sharpened," was the answer ; and the
servant shuffles on, without once looking at his
master, lest he should be suspected of loitering on
the way.   "Well, well, that is right, and see that
they are well sharpened, do you hear ? "   A few
minutes later, and an old woman hobbles by.
"Eh, you, where are you going to, my good
woman ? "   "To the dairy, to get some milk for
the lunch, your honour."   "Well, well," the squire

replies, "only see that none of the milk is spilt and wasted." "And you, Zacharka," he cries out directly after, "where are you sneaking off to, you lazy vagabond? I'll give you something to run for; that is the third time you have gone across the yard, and each time came back as empty-handed as you went. Get into the house, will you, and mind your work." And Zacharka obediently returns to his work, which consists in dozing at his post in the ante-room till his young master may happen to want him. The latter, when he is not in bed, spends his time in lounging on his wide soft sofa, to lie at full length on which is not, with him, a mere relaxation or enjoyment, but is his normal position. And close by its side are placed his slippers, so capacious and easy-fitting, that when he lets fall his feet from off the sofa on to the ground, they drop of themselves into them, without any trouble or effort on his part. Nor is the mistress of the house less busily engaged than the rest of the family. A large part of the morning is occupied in anxious consultation with one of the female serfs as to a jacket that is being made for the eldest son, and she herself measures it out with a piece of chalk, and sees it cut then and there, lest the girl should steal a strip of the cloth. Later on in the day she will, with

her husband, take a leisurely stroll through the
garden, and see what vegetables are fit to be
gathered, and what fruit is sufficiently ripe to be
plucked.   And then it is full time to prepare for
the great event of the day.   Each member of the
family is consulted as to what he would like for
dinner, and each has his favourite dish or sauce to
recommend, whilst fresh orders are being continu-
ally given as to how the cook is to flavour the soup,
or with what particular sauce he is to serve up the
meat and fowls.   After dinner, all enjoy a long
siesta, and for two or three hours the utmost quiet
prevails in the house as well as in the kitchen and
courtyard; and then a hearty substantial tea is
served, which disposed of, the family retire to rest,
and as they lay themselves down to sleep, they do
not fail to thank God that he has allowed them to
pass another day in undisturbed peace and tranquillity.   Once indeed this tranquillity was strangely
broken by the arrival of a letter, an unheard-of and
unprecedented event in the history of the Oblomoffs.   The envelope was curiously examined,
and turned over and over by every member of the
household in the vain endeavour to guess, by the
hand-writing, from whom the letter could have
come; and then, instead of being opened, was
placed on the mantelpiece for perusal on the

morrow, as it might contain bad news, and no one
could summon courage to unseal it, till every possible conjecture had been made as to what it might
be about. The next day, and for several weeks,
the letter formed the sole theme of conversation;
and only after numerous consultations was it
finally decided to pluck up heart, risk any danger,
and see what it really contained. It turned out
to be from an aunt, residing some hundred versts
distant, who prayed them to send her a particular
receipt for currant preserves. Of course, it was
decided that the required receipt should be copied
and forwarded. But each day something happened
to cause them to postpone writing till the morrow,
"and," adds the novelist, "though it is now more
than two years since the letter was received, I am
not sure that it has yet been answered."

The stolid apathy and fixed inactivity of an
Oblomoff will cease to provoke any feeling of sur-
prise on our part if we take into account the
social position he and his class occupied, and the
education he received. He was a *barine*—a
Russian word, which though always translated into
English by the term *gentleman*, has no equivalent
in our language—a kind of irresponsible *roi fainé-
ant* on his estate, and had at his beck and call, as
the novelist reminds us, "not one Zacharka, but

fifteen hundred Zacharkas," whose duty it was to
save their master every bother and care, and to
spare him the necessity of doing anything for himself that involved the slightest thought or the
least bodily movement. The conditions of his
life rendered any rational development of his intellectual or moral nature an impossibility. From
his infancy habituated to depend physically and
morally on the service and labour of others, he
naturally regarded work of any kind as a burden,
the necessary accompaniment of poverty and
serfdom, and could not imagine that a *barine*
would ever condescend to anything so low and
vulgar ; of course, he went to school, where he sat
quietly in class, listened to what the masters
taught, simply because he could not help doing
so, but took no interest in what he heard, and
looked on all study as a punishment inflicted
on men for the sin of their first parents. Nor did
he gain any good from his university career, his
head crammed with a mass of undigested knowledge, utterly unconscious of the necessity of
making that knowledge the rule and guide of
life. And if Oblomoff went through the routine
of school and college studies, he did so simply in
order that he might enter the Government service,
secure a rank, and—what constitutes the supreme

ambition of every true Russian—obtain the right
to wear a civil or military uniform; for we must
not forget that the universities and the higher
schools of Russia are not, as in Western Europe,
the products of slow spontaneous growth.   In
the beginning they were the artificial creations of
Government, and for a long time continued to
bear the distinctive character of establishments
founded for the sole purpose of supplying the
civil service with well-trained officials, providing
the public schools with teachers, and finding
instructed engineers and officers for the army and
navy.

But though Oblomoff instinctively hated work,
which, we are expressly told, he included together
with illness and poverty among the accidental evils
of life, he was not altogether devoid of the ambition
to do something for the general good and welfare of
men.   For several years he worked untiringly at a
new original plan, conceived in accordance with the
spirit of modern ideas for the better organisation
of his estate and the improvement of his peasants.
Every morning, directly he had slipped off his bed,
he would hurriedly drink his tea, and then at once
lie down on the sofa, his head propped up with a
cushion, and would think and think over his
scheme, till his head ached with the undue strain

of excessive work, and, murmuring to himself,
"Enough for to-day," he would fall asleep,
exhausted and worn out. Neither the love of
Olga, with her self-sacrificing eagerness to stir
Oblomoff from his apathy, nor the example of his
friend Stoltz, with his keen practical energy, could
overcome the moral fear that in reality forms the
fundamental trait in the character of Oblomoff.
As he lay stretched out on his sofa he could form
schemes and indulge in vague ideas of making his
life useful to others ; but the instant it came to
putting his plans into execution, he involuntarily
shrank from binding himself to any obligation, and
dreaded the possibility of becoming involved in disputes, difficulties, and strife. The stern realities of
life frightened him ; the devotion of an Olga lost
all its charms directly be perceived that it required
from him something else than a languid abandonment to sentiment ; the enterprising boldness of a
Stoltz shocked his shrinking sensitiveness. He
could not bring himself to act till he had considered and foreseen every possible issue of the
event, and thus a cowardly fear of failure unnerved
and paralysed his will.

A strained feeling of patriotism has led Peasareff and other critics to condemn Goncharoff for
portraying in the person of Stoltz, a German, the

man of action, the complete antithesis of Oblomoff. In like manner Tourgenieff was sharply
attacked, because in his novel " On the Eve,"
published in the same year as Goncharoff's
"Oblomoff," he has put Insaroff, the Bulgarian, in
opposition to the Russian Bersenieff. Such com-
plaints are essentially puerile; and we might just
as well blame the physician who determines the
illness from which his patient is suffering, as be
angry with Tourgenieff and Goncharoff for expos-
ing that terrible malady, Oblomoffism, which so
long spread its curse over the cultured classes of
Russia. And as we read these stories of an epoch
so near to us in time, so far removed from us in
every other respect, we notice two characteristics
common to all these Russian Oblomoffs. They
are but talkers, and nothing more; in their dissatisfaction at lacking the energy to accomplish all
they wish, they sullenly refrain from doing the
little that lies within their power; they let slip out
of their hands any favourable chance that may
occur; and it is by men of foreign origin and
education that the practical organisation of the
reforms they so eloquently advocate in words
is carried out. Bersenieff may plead in
glowing speech the cause of progress; but it is
Insaroff who proves in deed to be the true patriot,

and who in energy of character and singleness of
aim stands out in such marked contrast to these
empty talkers and parrot chatterers of social
philosophy and political economy.   Nay, they are
equally unable to manage their own private affairs.
Oblomoff may denounce, as he lolls on his sofa,
the dishonesty of Matveieff, who presents against
him a forged bill of exchange; but it is the
German Stoltz who forces the rogue to give it up
and secures his well-merited punishment.   We
further observe that, however loudly they may
preach and with whatever assurance they may lay
down the law, they never succeed in blinding the
quicker, sharper judgment of women, and their
hollow pretences are seen through and detected
by those whose good opinion and love they desire
to gain.   The kindlier qualities of an Oblomoff
may for awhile awaken Olga's sympathy, and
inspire her with the hope to stir him from his
aimless inertness, but his ignoble love of ease
prevents the hold which at one moment she
obtained over him being permanent or complete.
In the same way, it was impossible that Ellen could
find any real satisfaction in the empty theorisings
of the priggish orators by whom she was surrounded, and she only found her true province in
life when she made herself a co-worker in the

cause Insaroff had at heart, since, to use her own words, " he not only talks, but acts, and will act."

Of Goncharoff's three novels, " The Precipice " is the longest, and it must be confessed the weakest. Its cardinal fault, the want of historical unity, must be attributed to the long period, no less than twenty years, over which its composition extended. The pictures it gives of the past are drawn with that sureness of hand which never fails the author of "Oblomoff" when describing Russian life such as it was in the days of his youth and early manhood. Unfortunately, he has introduced characters that belong to a later period, and thus two different epochs are confusedly mingled. The work, we are told, is designed to represent the "awakening dawn," when Russia first awoke from her long sleep, and to depict the struggle between the old and the new. But the task is ill suited to the genius of Goncharoff, who does not possess that quick perception which enabled Tourgenieff to seize on and note every varying phase in the reform movement that agitated his country between the years 1860 and 1870. There is, accordingly, a want of completeness in the portrait of Mark Volochoff, who is intended to represent the new generation; the worse traits in his nature are dwelt upon with unnecessary emphasis, and there are glaring inconsistencies in the character as drawn by the novelist which it is impossible to reconcile.

We are told very little of the education or early training which had made Volochoff what he was when first introduced to us, already in his thirtieth year. We only know that he had been a student at the University of Moscow, which, however, he left without taking a degree ; that he served for a short time in the army, but soon got mixed up in some political affair, and was sent to live under police surveillance in a small remote provincial town. Here he quickly became the theme of gossiping wonder. His strange, uncouth manner and untidy dress, his offensive indifference to the requirements of the world, his outspoken contempt for the ordinary rules of morality, his ostentatious neglect of all religious observances, and his unconcealed hostility to any teaching that bore the taint of orthodoxy, rendered him an object of mingled curiosity and terror. The good people of Manielovka, where he took up his forced residence, listened to him in bewilderment as he set forth the "new faith" it was his mission to preach, and declared that henceforth the aim of every true and honest man should be to "clean the brain" of the rubbish that, accumulating for

centuries, had in the end effectually clogged the
healthy working of the human mind. But brain-
cleaning, though it may be an attractive, is certainly a dangerous operation, and requires a far
more delicate touch than the rough hand of a
Volochoff possessed. He led more than one of
those who allowed themselves to be attracted by
the daring novelty of his creed to the giddy precipice into which they threw what they fondly
believed were only childish prejudices, but the
loss of which involved the abandonment of all
faith in God and all belief in life.

It is evident that Goncharoff wished to make
the character of Volochoff unpleasing and anti-
pathetic. His rude speech and unpolished manners are calculated to repel. But I need scarcely
remark, these qualities are gratuitously assigned,
since a man may be the rankest materialist, and
yet be exemplary in his toilet and punctiliously
scrupulous in his observance of the drawing-room
code. We may acknowledge that Volochoff's
ideas on religion, honour, duty, and marriage
were a strange and contradictory medley of
opinions he had gained from an ill-digested study
of books he had read, but not understood; and
most of us, I presume, will reject his wild theory
of " free love," though his peculiar doctrine, it

would appear, has of late obtained acceptance in sober England. But when we have admitted all this, the errors of the man and his perverted views of life lend only an increased weight to the sentence of condemnation we must pass on that old sleepy Russia, of which Goncharoff is the kindly annalist. He is its creation, and the appearance of a Volochoff both marks the awakening of the country to the first glimmering consciousness of its responsibilities and duties, and is at the same time the just penalty it had to pay for its long slumberous indifference to the spiritual instincts of our nature.

LECTURE II.

IVAN SERGEIVITCH TOURGENIEFF.

No Russian writer, unless it be Count Tolstoi, ever enjoyed so undisputed and so widespread a popularity as that which fell to the lot of Tourgenieff. Each of his more important works has for its theme some burning question of the day, and consequently the publication of a new tale by Tourgenieff was always regarded as an event in the world of Russian letters, exciting no less keen an interest among those who shared the opinions he advocated than among those who were most opposed to his views. He was, moreover, the first who made Western Europe acquainted with the life of Russia and with the literature that life produced. His long residence in France brought him into communion with the best representatives of French thought ; the Russian mind and genius attracted first the curiosity and then the sympathy of men like Merimée; and his novels were translated and had already obtained a place in European literature when even the names of

his great contemporaries were unknown beyond
the limits of their country. Many misconceptions
and prejudices as to the character, belief, and
aims of the Russian people, once common to us
all, but now cherished only by the ignorant or assumed from a desire to secure the triumph of a
party creed, have been cleared up and removed
mainly through the closer and sounder knowledge
of Russia we have gained from the study of his
works. But, whilst freely acknowledging the high
service he rendered in this respect, we must not,
like many of his foreign critics, ignore the fact that,
though to the last his love for Russia was warm
and eager, with each year of his sojourn abroad,
his trust in the Russian people grew weaker, till
he would seem to have lost all belief that they
possessed the patient power, or anything beyond
the vague will, to work out their own destinies.

The novels of Tourgenieff form a sequel to those
of Goncharoff. They treat of two successive
periods through which newly-awakened Russia had
to pass. In "Roudine," " A Nobleman's Retreat,"
and "On the Eve," he has painted the age of
spouting theorisers, when the old order of things
had died out, but the new order had not yet taken
root,—an age of unrest that has been happily
baptised as the " castle-building epoch." In

"Fathers and Children," "Smoke," and "Virgin Soil," is sketched the age of action,—a period of practical patriotism that witnessed the temporary triumph of Slavophil ideas and the accomplishment of a series of wide reforms, which, but for the criminal folly of a small and unscrupulous party of noisy agitators, must have resulted in the final deliverance of the country from the hereditary shackles that had hitherto impeded her free and natural development. Taken together, these six novels present a general picture, or as Tourgenieff himself has expressed it, a "concentrated reflection" of the most critical moments in the social history of contemporary Russia. The period of which they treat is so near to us that, perhaps, we have little reason to be surprised if they have been made the subject of hot and bitter controversy, or if, with few exceptions, his Russian critics, while admitting their artistic excellences, have distorted their real teaching in obedience to the exigencies of party spirit. Fortunately for us, we, as foreigners, have no reason to yield to any such temptation, and can, with strictest impartiality, criticise them from the point of view which their writer assures us he consistently maintained throughout the whole of his literary career. "The author of 'Roudine,' written in 1855," we read in his

introduction to the collected edition of his works,
"and the author of 'Virgin Soil,' written in 1876,
is one and the same man. In the whole course of
these years, I have endeavoured, as far as my
power and knowledge permitted me, conscien-
tiously and truthfully to represent and to incarnate
what Shakspere has called the body and pressure
of the age, and to catch and to reflect the quickly-
changing features of the cultured class of Russian
society, which has mainly formed the theme of my
observation and study." These words admirably
explain the source of Tourgenieff's popularity, and
at the same time mark the limit of his genius.
Then, even more than now, the reading public of
Russia was composed of the class Tourgenieff
himself belonged to. No wonder, then, if they
gave their love to one who, alone of all the writers
of his age, remained faithful to the literary traditions in which they had been bred, who reproduced in prose the choice artistic language of a
Poushkin, and who, in style, thought, and tone, was
a full and sympathetic representative and interpreter of the culture which constituted the basis
and foundation of their life. It may seem that
the outward form adopted by a writer is of
secondary importance, but I think that Tourgenieff's
relation to the people, and particularly to their

religious faith, may be best explained by his tenacious adherence to the literary style of the past. The absence of all affectation in their life and speech, their simple uninquiring faith in God, their patient endurance of wrong, their cheerful submission to poverty, suffering, or illness, and, above all, the tranquil, uncomplaining spirit in which they meet death, these and like traits in the character of the Russian people are brought out by Tourgenieff with supreme realistic force. But it is impossible not to remark that much of this simplicity strikes the novelist as strange and in-harmonious with that culture he had learned to worship; and it may be safely said that he never more than partially realised those hidden forces in the Russian people, which are entirely remote from and unintelligible to Western European civilisation, but are closely connected with their religious creed, and, when allowed their full play, will enable them to work out their future inde-pendently of foreign influences. It is very different with writers like Dostoevsky and Tolstoi, who find in their religious belief a tie that binds them to the people closely in soul and mind, and gives strength to their conviction that the aspirations common to them and the people alike will, in spite of all temporary hindrances and disappoint-

ments, be eventually realised. For this reason
Tourgenieff has never been a power in Russian
literature. His novels are eagerly read, their high
moral tone and perfect finished style are recognised
and admired, but, whilst tracing its newest depar-
tures and fresh currents, he has never guided or
controlled the tendencies of Russian life and
thought. Wedded to his Western European
theories, he could find no sure holding-point in
national self-development, and would seem to have
thought that Russian progress consists in a more
or less successful imitation of a civilisation that
has nothing in common with Russian traditions
and can never contribute to the natural and healthy
growth of the Russian people.

After what I have already said in my last lecture
respecting the novels of Goncharoff, it will scarcely
be necessary to dwell at any length on Tourgenieff's
" Roudine." He already belongs to the past.
Useful in his generation, he appears to us of a later
day to be a mere phrasemaker, a " minikin Ham-
let," as Tourgenieff calls him. The eloquent zeal
with which the young orator pleads for the reform
of abuses has lost the charm that once made him
the hero of drawing-rooms, and won for him the
easy admiration of sentimental women, who hung
upon his every word and took his fervid declama-

tion for genuine coin. At the same time, he is
better than Oblomoff, and his impulsive advocacy
of right and justice compares favourably with
Oblomoff's sofa musings on the unredressed
wrongs and evils of life. But, after all, the one
only dreams and the other only talks. His real
worthlessness comes out most strongly if we contrast Roudine with the landed gentry of his neighbourhood, such as Pegasoff, on whom he looked
down as beings of an inferior order. We shall
then see that a very imperfect activity may be less
hurtful than Roudine's barren eloquence. We
know that Pegasoff was guilty of taking bribes, did
not scruple to toady his superiors, and professed
a worldly disbelief in honesty and disinterestedness.
But his peasants were not so neglected as those
on Roudine's estate, of whose existence, except
through the monthly reports of his German
steward, their master was completely ignorant.
For, like all men of his class, Roudine considered
himself to be far above the common tribe; and
as Dobrolouboff, the great Russian critic, has well
expressed it, "in the days of Roudine, men who
believed themselves to be superior to the sphere
in which they were fated to move, grew so fast and
multiplied with such rapidity, that, if the change
that came over the national life had not happily

put a stop to their growth, there would soon have been no sphere left for them to be superior to." Only once does he escape from his habitual sin of believing mere words to have a healing power, and this one instance of activity affords a striking proof of the absence of solidity of character, without which the best· of our ῾deeds are but irrational impulse. He takes part in the Parisian Revolution of 1848, and dies of a wound received whilst defending one of the barricades. As if his own country had no need of the services of her children, and as if there was no cause save the stranger's on which to exercise his energies !

Roudine's fatal mistake consisted in that, whilst he interested the mind and stirred the ideas of men, he forgot that, if he would achieve any practical῾good, it was necessary to touch the heart and appeal to the feelings. It was impossible that men who had nothing better than fine-spun theories to offer, who were always preparing themselves and getting ready, but never put their hand boldly to work, could long be accepted as authorities and guides. Oblomoff had to give way to Roudine, and Roudine, in his turn, is replaced by Lavretsky, the hero of Tourgenieff's next novel, " A Nobleman's Retreat." Unlike Roudine, Lavretsky is not of unmixed noble descent, his

father having married a serf-girl, and he more than
once boasts that "pure plebeian blood flows in
his veins." It is this plebeian descent that inspires
him with a belief in the youth and strength of his
country, encourages his hope in the continuous
development of national life, and causes him to
distrust the abstract reasoning and ideal concep-
tions of a perfect state of society in which Roudine
liked to indulge. It is true that his marriage with
the heartless and frivolous Barbara, so soon followed
by the discovery of his wife's unfaithfulness, induced
him for a while to renounce all work, and, in the
solitude and quiet of his country home, to seek
forgetfulness of the past. But that which would
have lulled Roudine into sluggish resignation,
aroused Lavretsky to a consciousness of the
humiliation involved in any such passive surrender
to fate, and in all around him, in every mood of
nature, he found a fresh stir to activity. It was
thus that, on the first day of his arrival in the
dull country village where he had resolved to bury
himself from the world, the tranquil languor of the
scenery seemed to typify only too faithfully the
dead calm and purposeless stagnation of the days
that awaited him. " There was not a breath of
air or the least noise to break the calm. The
wind had not strength enough to stir the foliage of

the trees ; the swallows, as they swept the ground
with their wings, silently chased one another, and
the heart felt oppressed with the silent persistence
of their flight.   The sun sank softly in the clear
blue sky ; the clouds floated slowly in the golden
ether, alone seeming to have an aim, and to know
whither they were bound.   Elsewhere, and at this
very moment, the sea of life was tossing with its
foaming and tumultuous waves ; but here it was
calm and motionless as a piece of stagnant water."
And whilst he thus gazed at the clouds, which
" knew whither they were bound," he resolved to
make himself an aim and to find a purpose for his
life.   As we might expect, the end is not easily
attained, but, though its achievement is marred by
occasional failures, he finally conquers, and listening to the counsel of the pure and noble-minded
Liza, finds strength sufficient to forego the rich
store of happiness his love for her promised to
secure him, and, in obedience to her prayer, consents to pardon the wife who has done him so cruel
a wrong.   Nor, after his forgiveness of Barbara, does
he repeat the error he had committed when, smarting under the treachery of his wife, life seemed to
have lost every purpose and every charm ; but,
instead of weakly hugging his grief to his heart, he
puts aside self, and seeks consolation for his own

woes in ameliorating the ills of others, and in im-
proving the lot of his peasants.   The fate of the
two heroes, Roudine and Lavretsky, is equally
tragic.   But, whilst the death of the one, with its
flaunting theatrical surroundings, excites within us
a mingled feeling of regret and discontented contempt for the man who thus wilfully threw away
his life, as we follow Lavretsky in his new career
of activity, and see how he preserved to the last
his belief in good and firmness of will, though we
pity him in his disappointed search after happiness,
we can never despise him.

The title of Tourgenieff's novel, "On the Eve,"
sufficiently characterises the stage in Russian
development immediately succeeding the Oblomoff, Roudine, and Lavretsky periods.   The
action of the story is laid in 1853, and none of
the epochs sketched by Tourgenieff in his preceding novels afforded such rich and varied materials
as those days of ardent hope and expectation.
Russia has produced many striking and original
individualities, but in her history we find few great
epochs, and not one that can be compared with
this era of eager palpitating life, revelling in the
consciousness of youthful strength, and longing to
put forth its hitherto unexercised powers.   The
keynote to the whole work, and which is sustained

throughout from the first to the last page, is given
in one of the earlier scenes, where Schoubine says
to his friend Bersenieff, "But go, pray go; I was
only talking so, and do not wish to keep you : be off
into the garden as quickly as you like : you will find
Ellen there : apparently she is waiting for you, in
any case she is waiting for somebody; do you understand the meaning of those words,—she is waiting?"

Like Ellen, Russia was unquiet, dissatisfied, on
the eve of breaking with a sluggish, unproductive
past, awaiting the advent of men who should be
able to satisfy her newly-awakened aspirations.
But where could such men be found? Certainly
not among the Loupoyaroffs, the empty, frivolous
expounders of the political creed of young Russia,
or even in a Bersenieff or a Schoubine. Bersenieff
is filled with an unselfish devotion to all that is
good, and indulges in the dream of a happier
future for his country. But his heroism is of a
passive nature ; he is able to endure much, to
make great sacrifices, and to behave nobly when
an occasion presents itself. The occasion, however, must come unsought. He cannot determine
a line of action, or play an independent part when
called upon to act. Schoubine puts to himself,
and to others, the question, "Whether the time
will ever come when we shall have real men

amongst us?" and, having posed the question, languidly falls back into his wonted caustic indifference. Of all the characters introduced into the novel, Insaroff is the only one who does not talk, but acts; and he is not a Russian, but a Bulgarian. He is strong exactly in those points where these Russian theorists are weak. A Bulgarian by birth, he is filled with a passionate love for his country,—a love strengthened by the desire to avenge the brutal murder of his mother by a Turkish *aga*, and the not less brutal execution of his father for having slain the assassin; and he lives with but one object,—to secure its freedom from the foul tyranny of the Turks. He never thinks of separating his personal happiness from the happiness of his country. Such an idea, however natural to the educated and philosophical Bersenieff, never occurs to the simple-minded Bulgarian, and in promoting the one, he believes he is best promoting the other.

"You love your country dearly?" is the question Ellen asks him in one of their earlier interviews.

"What else is there worth loving?" he hotly replies. "What else is there which never changes, of which you never doubt, in which, next to God, you never cease to believe? And when she, your country, has need of you ... well, well, the veriest boor, the lowest beggar in Bulgaria, not one whit less than I myself, awaits one and the same thing : we have all but one and the same end in view."

In these words we see the whole difference between the two men. Insaroff is no cold philosopher, dreamingly wondering whether he shall ever be called on to play a part in the struggle for national freedom, and, if so, what part it will be. That events must decide; enough for him that he be allowed to enlist, in the van or in the rear, in the coming battle against wrong and injustice. Bersenieff, too, is capable of this, but he would be glad were the sacrifice never demanded of him, and looks forward with shrinking and aversion to the possibility of being engaged in the strife. In her journal, Ellen, with the keenness of a woman's judgment, notes this inferiority in Bersenieff's character: " He is, perhaps, more learned and wiser; this may be ; but he is so little when compared with *him*. Whenever *he* speaks of his fatherland, his form becomes fuller, his face wears a strange beauty, and his voice obtains a manlier tone· Then, in truth, there is not a man in the whole world to whom he need yield."

And this contrast between the Bulgarian patriot and the'Russian political spouters, is brought out, with a force that is almost stern in its pointedness, in the scene where the dying Insaroff, the man of action, is visited by Loupoyaroff, the frothy declaimer: "Insaroff was tired out with this unexpected visit, and lay down on the sofa. 'And that,' he muttered bitterly, as he looked up at Ellen, 'is our rising generation, our young Russia! They give themselves grand airs, and talk wonderfully well, but it is all talk, and there it ends.'"

We can, then, easily understand why, after Insaroff's death, Ellen feels that she has no country but his, and determines to remain faithful to the cause to which he had devoted his life. "Return to Russia?" she writes. "Why? What is there to do in Russia?"

And the very last sentence in the book forms a sad, but just, commentary on Ellen's despairing query. Urban Ivanovitch, her great-uncle, has received a letter from Schoubine, in which his correspondent repeats his favourite question as to whether there is any just ground to hope that real men will ever rise up amongst us. "And as he read these lines, Urban Ivanovitch played with his fingers, and with a puzzled glance looked out of the window of his room."

And soon, even whilst puzzled Urbans were still playing with their fingers, idly renouncing as impossible the task of solving the destinies of the

Russian people, these "real men" appeared, or those who gave themselves out as such,—men who claimed to know in what the malady of their country consisted, and who at once set to work, without caring to pose as propagandists of any particular creed, new or old. What that work was, and how they sought to carry it out, forms the theme of Tourgenieff's greatest and most famous novel, "Fathers and Children." Its publication provoked much bitter controversy, the echoes of which have even yet scarcely died away, and its author, so long the idol of Russian youth, was roundly accused of having calumniously caricatured the rising generation. Whether there was any real ground for this ill-feeling, the source of which, I believe, is to be found in the suspicious and distrustful attitude the novelist assumes in reference to the more prominent phases of contemporary Russian life, we shall be best able to judge after we have made ourselves acquainted with the subject and leading personages of the story.

Its characters naturally fall into two groups, and nearly the whole book is made up of scenes in which the representatives of the old and new school are brought into collision. To the former belong Nicholas Petrovitch Kirsanoff and his brother,

Paul Petrovitch; to the latter Arcadie, the son of
Nicholas, and his friend, Bazaroff, the son of an
old army surgeon   It is worthy of remark that, as
in his "Stories from a Sportsman's Note-book,"
Tourgenieff did not fill in his picture of country life,
such as it was in the olden days, with portraits of serf-
owners exceptionally coarse or cruel, but rather
selected the better types of their class, so now, he
does not fail to attribute to the two "fathers,"
among the qualities inherited from their social
position, many traits of a pleasing and even praise-
worthy kind.   But in both cases the conclusion
we are forced to draw is one and the same.   We
feel that these men have outlived their age;
neither in sympathies, feelings, nor ideas, do they
belong to the present, and, in their unwilling concessions to the spirit of progress, tacitly acknowledge
that they have no interest or part in the work of
the new generation.   Nothing is allowed to disturb
the monotony of their lives ; and if, under some
strong external pressure, they are momentarily
roused from their inactive lethargy, the result of
their spasmodic activity is barren and unproductive.

"Every one knows me to be a liberal and a
lover of progress," complacently urges Paul
Petrovitch.   "And why am I so?   Because I
honour the aristocracy.   Where there is no feeling

of self-respect, and this feeling is most highly developed among the aristocracy, there can be no durable foundation for *le bien public*."

Perfectly satisfied that he has well proved the sincerity of his sympathy with his age by the utterance of this profound truth, and by condescendingly dubbing himself a liberal, the good Paul, as he lounges in his easy-chair, contentedly passes the years of his life, which indeed go by pleasantly enough, since, as the novelist maliciously observes, "nowhere does time fly so quickly as in Russia." And if occasionally he gets angry with the new-fangled exigencies made on him and his class, we can easily understand, and almost excuse, his petulant regret for the old days when he and his compeers were allowed to sleep through their lives in a slumber of unbroken content.

In stern contrast with these form-worshippers and word-idolaters stands out the commanding figure of Bazaroff, the self-reliant and self-concentred realist. There is a strength and power in Bazaroff which none can resist; however prejudiced we may be against the creed he professes, and however repelled we may be by his habitual roughness of conduct and speech, we are involuntarily attracted towards him, and though there is, apparently, nothing striking or brilliant about

him, he none the less towers above all the other
characters of the novel, and forms its one central
point of interest. At the same time, of all the
persons introduced into the romance, he is the
most Russian. His speech is characterised by a
simplicity, pointedness, and mocking humour that
at once betray his true Russian nature and training. Better than any of them he knows how to
speak to the peasant, and it is in him, rather than
in any of the others, that the *moujik* is most ready
to recognise a fellow-countryman. And the interest which he excites in us is unsought and
extorted in spite of ourselves; for, whilst he concerns himself but little, or not at all, with the
thoughts and pursuits of others, all are strangely
occupied with what he thinks or does.

We are told but little of Bazaroff's previous life,
and this silence on the part of the novelist as to
the experiences and mental process by which he
became a negationist, has been attributed by some
of his critics to the spirit of antipathy which, as
they allege, colours the whole portrait. It is
against this accusation that Tourgenieff somewhat
warmly defends himself in his " Literary and Personal Reminiscences," published seven years later.
" Probably my readers will be astonished, if I tell
them that all the time I was writing the novel I

felt a kind of involuntary attraction to Bazaroff, and that, with the exception of his views on art, I share nearly all his opinions." It seems to me, then, that the reason why Tourgenieff has not introduced any details concerning Bazaroff's earlier life and education is that his object was, not to give the whole career of the man, with those changes in character and modifications in opinion which we all experience, but rather to sketch one single stage, and that the most important and the most interesting, in his mental and spiritual development. Nor does the portrait, through being painted on a narrower canvas, lose in fulness. On the contrary, the entire man appears before us, drawn with a completeness that renders each little trait known and familiar.

Like all Russians who claim to be the intellectual leaders of their generation, Bazaroff is a theorist. The peculiar conditions of Russian society and its government render it impossible that they should take any active part in the life surrounding them. To do this, they would have to cast away that which is most precious to them, —independence of thought,—and, losing all self-activity, sink into obedient and well-drilled workers of the bureaucratic machine. But, unlike most of them, Bazaroff is possessed with an ardent,

unconquerable desire to work ; his theory is based
on this demand, and his nature is such that he
cannot help seizing on any chance opportunity
that may be afforded him of putting it, however
imperfectly, into practice. For he is thoroughly
in earnest, and it is to this earnestness we should
attribute those peculiar traits in his character
which, on a first acquaintance, are calculated to
shock and repel. His ideas, and the way he
insists upon them, as if no one but a fool
could think of disputing them, are marked by a
sharp narrowness, a contemptuous hostility to
received opinions, and a rough indifference to the
prejudices of others, that is apt to make him
imperious and overbearing. But he is by no
means a dry pedant, with whom logic has taken
the place of feeling, and who, having solved a
question abstractedly and without reference to
those it closely concerns, thinks he has done all
that is necessary, and finds full satisfaction and
contentment in the solution arrived at. Hence
he is easily excited, can ill brook contradiction,
and, in spite of his consciousness that truth
should be advocated calmly and judiciously, will
frequently, for the sake of surprising and crushing
an antagonist, indulge in violent tirades, and give
utterance to the most extravagant paradoxes. It

is in this spirit that he denounces Poushkin and his poetry as "all nonsense," declares "a good chemist to be twenty times more useful than the greatest of poets," and, on one occasion, breaks out into a vehement protest against the doctrine of self-sacrifice for the good of others. "I recollect," he says, "you told me this morning, as we were passing Philip's white pretty cottage, that Russia would only then be what she should be, when the last *moujik* had such a home, and that each one of us should help to bring about such a state of things. Now, I tell you, I hate this last *moujik* of yours, this Philip, or what not, for whom I am to work and sweat till I wear my skin away, and who will never thank me for what I do; and, indeed, why should he? And so, he will live in his pretty white cottage, and I,—well, I shall die, perish, and rot into nothing; the fate common to us all."

Though little prone to parade his plebeian descent, Bazaroff never conceals it, and even regards his humble birth with a pride equal to that which the haughtiest noble takes in his aristocratic origin. "My grandfather ploughed his own land," he tells Paul Petrovitch. And precisely because Bazaroff was not a *baritch*,—the son of a noble,—he enjoyed the trust and confidence of the peasantry, and was enabled to practise in his dealings with them a frankness that would have been taken in ill part from one of gentle birth. Paul Petrovitch could not understand that it is possible for a man to be at one with the people and still have contempt for the degrading superstitions that in the course of ages have overcrusted their simple creed. "No, no," he petulantly exclaims, "I will not believe that you gentlemen really know the Russian people, —that you are the representatives of their wants, their longings. The Russian people are not such as you imagine. They honour tradition, they are patriarchal, they cannot live without faith."

"I will not dispute that," interrupted Bazaroff; "I am even ready to grant that on this point you are right."

"And if I am right?"

"Still that proves nothing."

"How, proves nothing?" stammered the astonished Paul Petrovitch; "then you go against the people?"

"And what if we do? The peasant believes that, when it thunders, the prophet Elijah is riding through the sky in his chariot. Am I to agree with him? Besides, if he is a Russian, am I not one also?"

"No, you are not a Russian, after all that you have said! I cannot acknowledge you to be a Russian."

"My grandfather ploughed his own land," answered Bazaroff, haughtily. "Ask any of your peasants, in which of us two he sees a fellow-countryman. Why, you do not know even how to speak to him."

"And you speak to him, and at the same time despise him!"

"Why not, if he deserves contempt?"

Bazaroff is the uncompromising foe of all shams and of everything bearing the taint of pretence. He never affects to be different to, or better than, what he really is. He may be unintelligible to men like Paul Petrovitch, the rule of whose lives is based on decorous prudery; but the genuineness of his speech is readily recognised by those who, from their position, have never been corrupted by the false shows of society. "He belongs to us and is one of ourselves," exclaims an old serf.

This enmity to display not only colours the practical life of Bazaroff, but is equally evident in his relations to nature, poetry, and art. Nothing is valuable in his eyes unless it brings some tangible and calculable good. He acknowledges only that which he can touch with his hands, see with his eyes, taste with his tongue; in a word, what is cognisable to one or other of the senses. The rest of our feelings he attributes to the action of our nervous system, to be repressed and conquered rather than cultivated or encouraged. It is, therefore, impossible for him to find' pleasure in mere views of nature, in the harmony of music, in the colouring of the painter, in the rhyme of the poet, or in the charm of woman's beauty. For him there is no ideal beyond the real; aspirations towards something purer than earth of itself can afford are to him romantic and sentimental; he never looks beyond the human, or busies himself with those dreams of the spiritual, wherein so many find their best consolation. "The one important thing is that two and two make four," he declares; "all the rest is vain and empty." Here we have Bazaroff's prosaic view of the world and of human life. "Nature," he continues, "is not a temple, but a workshop, in which man is the workman." This forms the practical side of his creed. Worship of nature is an idle superstition; poetical delineations of nature are condemned as sentimental; the circle of his studies is limited to the real and positive, discarding all that lies beyond the province of experience and

proof. Hence, also, the realism which characterises his political opinions and speculations.
To none of those fine-sounding phrases which
Paul Petrovitch was pleased to parade before him
could he attach any solid, tangible signification.
" Aristocracy, liberalism, progress, principles," he
exclaims, " what a host of foreign and useless
words! A Russian has no need of them, and
should not accept them as a gift." And in speaking thus, Bazaroff is only protesting, perhaps too
angrily, against that monkey imitation of Western
Europe which so long impeded all national development in Russia, and could achieve nothing
better than the reproduction of foreign manners
and institutions on a soil unsuited to their growth.

Although, as I have said, Tourgenieff is
pointedly silent as to the youth and education of
Bazaroff, we can have no doubt as to some of the
controlling influences that caused him to put himself in antagonism to the conventional opinions
of his age. "At the present time," he explains,
" the most useful thing is denial, and so we
deny." He saw around him a noisy crowd of
preachers of liberalism, flaunting the borrowed
robes of French freethinkers, but in whose voice
the ring of insincerity, and in whose step the strut
and gait of men playing a part could easily be

detécted. The barrenness of their utterances was
emphasised by the ready glibness with which they
aired theories they neither cared nor tried to put
into practice. What wonder, then, if he turned
from these pretentious theorists in contempt, and,
in his hatred of mere words, set to "clearing
the ground" of antiquated prejudices and worn-
out creeds? The task of construction might be
left to others, but the first and most pressing need
was to find the solid rock on which to raise a
surer building than that which was already
toppling about their ears. We must not be surprised if he was over-passionate or somewhat
indiscriminate in his work of destruction. Has
not Swift, in his "Tale of a Tub," told us that
"zeal is never so highly obliged as when you set
it a-tearing." Besides, the system of serfdom had
struck too deeply into the social life of Russia to
permit of men destroying it without at the same
time uprooting some of the most cherished institutions of the past. He consequently called
himself, and is called by others, a Nihilist. The
name has, unfortunately, acquired a terrible and
evil meaning since Tourgenieff's novel was written.
But we should be doing a manifest injustice to
Bazaroff, were we to suppose that the policy he
advocated had anything in common with the

follies and extravagances of his professed followers, who have usurped the title to themselves,
and, by rendering it a synonym for assassin, have
made it an offence to every honest man.   Bazaroff
is a Nihilist in the sense of one "who bows before
no authority, accepts of no principle improved,
and looks at everything from a critical point of
view." He is thus the representative of his age,
and, however we may be displeased or irritated,
we must be content to make the best of him.
"For if," as M. Peasareff has well said, "Baza-
roffism be a malady, it is the malady of our days,
so widely spread that, in spite of all our pal-
liatives or amputations, we must learn to endure
it as well as we can. We may call it a good or an
evil, as we like ; but stay its progress we cannot,
for it pervades the very air we breathe."

What, then, is it that, in spite of the coldness
of his creed, and the harsh rejection he preaches
of the tenderer instincts of human nature, draws
us to Bazaroff, and causes us, I will not say to
tolerate and respect, but to sympathise with and
love him ? The man is terribly sincere in all that
he professes, but none the less he is, like most of
us, better than his creed. He struggles against
what he believes to be childish weaknesses, and
scorns as a treachery to his higher nature every

exhibition of love or care for others; and the
severity of the struggle against what he regards to
be a surrender of principle, only serves to proclaim
the strength and loftiness of his character.   Of
this we have a striking illustration in his affection
for his aged parents.   He inveighs against what
he calls "pampering the old people," and spends
as little of his time as possible at home, seizing
any pretext to stay with one or another of his
friends, since only thus can he pursue his studies
without perpetual interruption.   "At home it is
impossible to do anything," he explains to
Arcadie; "here at least you can shut yourself up
and work.   My father, it is true, tells me his room
is at my service, but never likes me to be out of
his sight.   And I am ashamed to close the door
on the old man.   And it is the same with mother.
I hear her groaning and sighing in the next room,
and then I have to leave off and go to her, and...
how refuse her?"   There is a kindliness of feeling in these words that belies the cold sternness
of his scientific rules of life.   And the half shame
with which he thus yields to the influence of our
common nature is altogether abandoned when,
brought face to face with death, he first feels the
real power of that love he had sought to deny.
He reminds his weeping father and mother that

now is the moment to prove the faith which they
have all their lives professed; and, when they
hesitatingly beseech him to avail himself of the
last consolations of religion, he consents, if, by so
doing, "he can only please them."

From Bazaroff's point of view, any such surrender to the natural promptings of his heart was
a proof of moral weakness; but, had he not been
blinded by a belief in his freedom from what he
looked upon as failing in others, these moments of
supposed weakness might have discovered to him
the cardinal error of the creed he had adopted.
Man is not sufficient in himself, and cannot with
impunity ignore the eternal principles of life.
Art, poetry, love,—the permanent elements of the
temporary,—may be denied in words; but they
irrevocably revenge themselves on those who deny
them, and make their power to be felt. We recognise the grandeur of Bazaroff's aims, but,
though he is head and shoulders above all who
surround him, whilst we admit their inferiority, we
are conscious that in them there is something
higher than Bazaroff, something to which mere
negation could never bring him. This something
is the life that animates them, and the human
elements of their feelings raise them above him.
To try and find a political tendency in the novel

is to misconceive its real meaning.   The passage
from the old to the new, this is but the scaffolding,
as it were, of the romance.   It has a deeper inner
lesson, and teaches the necessity of recognising
the one eternal law that runs through the ever
varying order of the world, as generation succeeds
to generation, exhibiting itself in different forms,
but in essence ever the same.   I ought rather to
have said this lesson is suggested by the novelist.
For, as M. Strachoff has pointed out in his
"Critical Essays on Tourgenieff and Tolstoi," if
Bazaroff disdainfully turns away from nature,
Tourgenieff refrains from reproaching him, but
silently sketches some picture of nature in which
are unfolded all her charms and beauties that
speak to the soul of man. · Bazaroff despises
friendship, and again he does not blame him, but
gives some fresh instance of trusting unselfish
devotion on the part of Arcadie to the very man
that ridicules all show of affection.   It is the
same with his denial of the parental tie and his
alienation from the life around him.   No judgment is pronounced upon him, but the novelist
brings us into the home of the old Bazaroffs, with
all their tender love and care for the son of whom
they are so proud.

We cannot but regret that Tourgenieff in his

later stories, "Smoke" and "Virgin Soil," did not
preserve the same calmness of tone towards what
he believed to be the errors and extravagances of
the new generation. Unfortunately, he would
seem to have felt too deeply the injustice of many
of the criticisms made on his "Fathers and
Children," and the two novels bear unpleasing
traces of his irritation. In both there is much to
anger and annoy. The attack on the hopes and
aims of young Russia is partial and passionate;
the types introduced to represent its ideas are
over-coloured to such an extent that they frequently
sink into caricatures; and it may be questioned
whether Bazaroff himself could be more negative
or more destructive than Potooguin, the novelist's
mouthpiece. Nor do his violent diatribes possess
one half the force that resided in those silent con-
demnations which Tourgenieff passed on the new
tendencies of Russian life and thought, when he
put in opposition to Bazaroff's wholesale denial
of nature, poetry, and art, their unrecognised
power over the soul of the man who vainly rebelled
against them. Much of the bitterness that
characterises his attack on the new departure in
Russian life contemporary with the appearance of
his novel must be attributed to his long residence
abroad, during which he had become saturated

with ideas that rendered it impossible for him to form a fair estimate of the equally rapid and startling changes effected in the political and social position of his country. In his eyes Russian social life has no solid foundation, and is so undermined with evils inherited from a system of privileged corruption, that it can afford no scope for healthy development and growth. "The wind has changed and chopped round to another quarter" complains Lietvinoff, the hero of the tale entitled "Smoke," "but, just as before, Russian life remains the same unsettled, feverish, profitless game of chance. Smoke, smoke!" he repeated many times; and forthwith everything seemed to him to be nothing but smoke,—his own life, Russian life, everything human, especially everything Russian! He called to mind all that had passed under his eyes during the last few years, not without thunder and great tumult. "Smoke!" he muttered, "smoke!" He called to mind the disorderly discussions, the noise in Goubareff's rooms, the disputes of other people, high and low, progressive and retrograde, old and young. "Smoke!" he repeated, "smoke and vapour!" He remembered the famous picnic, the remarks and speeches of great statesmen, and even everything that Potooguin had extolled; and it was all smoke, and nothing more!

In reply to this fierce diatribe, we may remark
that, if in truth the new life of Russia be nothing
but smoke, there is no great reason why it should
make the novelist so angry ; since, like all smoke,
it will be blown away by the first strong breeze,
and leave the ground clear for fresh workers
But Tourgenieff was right in declaring that "the
wind had changed." Russians have ceased to
be what they term Westerners, that is, admiring
imitators of Western Europe, and have become
Slavophils, that is, have found in their own country
and in their own people a higher object of worship
and devotion. They no longer believe that their
chief aim should be " to saunter Europe round, and
gather every vice in every ground," but have
accepted the healthier doctrine that each people
should work out their civilisation in harmony with
the traditions of their past. And if there be
confusion and chaos in their first efforts to find a
sure and solid basis whereon to build, and if in
their political programme there be much that is
extravagant and, it may be, absurd, this by no
means proves that their hopes and belief are
nothing more than empty, vaporous smoke.
Confusion must reign for awhile till life has re-
covered from the shock given to it. The waters
may be troubled, but the healing power of liberty

will in due time be felt, and the storm of conflict give place to the reign of stable order and peace. In spite of all hindrances, and though their work has been sadly thwarted and retarded by the criminal excesses of men who have not scrupled to cloak their selfish ends under the sacred name of patriotism, none can doubt the final victory and triumph of their cause. Least of all, should we English, so proud of our historical traditions, and the sworn foes of all that threatens or contravenes them, mock at those, who, like ourselves, are inspired with a faith in national life and progress, which no sarcasms of a Lietvinoff can destroy, or even impair.

In his latest work, "Short Poems in Prose," Tourgenieff has given us a fable, which, though of course originally written with a quite different intention, may, I think, be applied to the Slavophils, and be made the expression of the fearless spirit in which they labour, and are ready to labour, in carrying out their work to a successful end. "What a trifle will sometimes give new life to a man! I was one day walking along a road, lost in thought. Suddenly I raised my head. Before me lay the long straight road that ran between two rows of high poplar trees. And across it,—across this same road, about ten steps off, in the bright summer sunshine, a long train of sparrows was hopping, quickly, boldly, without fear. One in particular attracted my attention by its pompous strut, as it stretched out its beak, and chirped defiantly, as though it feared neither man nor devil. It had all the airs and importance of a conquering general on his march. And, in the meantime, high up in the sky, wheeled a huge vulture, that very likely would, ere long, pounce down and gulp up my swaggering hero. I curiously watched the scene with no little amusement, shook myself together, and got rid of my gloomy thoughts. In a moment, I felt arise within me, a boldness, a daring, a desire to live. And now, I thought, let my vulture, if it chooses, wheel its threatening flight over me. Never mind, we will have a fight for it yet ! "

LECTURE III.

THEODORE MICHAELOVITCH DOSTOEVSKY.

PART I.

THERE are few pages in the history of modern literature more heroically touching than those devoted to the story of the life of the great Russian novelist, Theodore Michaelovitch Dostoevsky. The son of a poor staff-surgeon, he was born in one of the Moscow hospitals, where his father served, on October 30, 1821. Together with his two brothers, Michael and André, he was brought up with strict but loving care, and till his fifteenth or sixteenth year was educated at home. The father himself undertook the Russian and Latin lessons, whilst masters from the different public schools were engaged to teach the boys French, German, history, arithmetic, and religion. The evenings were generally spent in reading aloud some novel or poem, the father and mother taking part; and it is interesting to note that Scott, Cooper, and De Foe, with Poushkin and Foukovsky, were special favourites. Like most future writers, Dostoevsky from an early age was fond of trying his hand at original compositions, and would frequently dramatise any story that had caught his fancy. The summer months were always spent on the small family estate in the government of Toula, and, during his stays in the country, the boy liked to associate and chat with the peasants, many of whom he has introduced into his different tales and novels. In 1837, a few months after the death of the mother, he was sent up to St. Petersburg and placed in the Engineers' School, where he remained till 1841, when, his father having died in the meantime, he entered the military service with the rank of sub-lieutenant. He was, however, little suited to such a career, being equally averse to the routine of military duties and the gay noisy life led by the majority of his fellow-officers; and three years later he finally quitted the army, and determined to devote himself exclusively to the literary profession.

It was in 1846 that he began writing his first novel, " Poor People." Its publication was attended with all those difficulties a poor unknown writer has usually to contend with. " When I finished it," Dostoevsky tells us, " I did not know what to do with it, or to whom to send it." The

only literary acquaintance he had in the world was
Grigorovitch, who, like his friend, was then beginning his career, and in great trouble to find an
editor, who would undertake to print his story,
"The Village." He promised to show the manuscript to Nekrasoff, the poet, then collecting
materials for an annual, which he proposed to
publish in January of the following year. Nekrasoff consulted with Belinsky as to the merits of
the tale, and M. Annenkoff, in his interesting
"Memoirs," has described the impression its
perusal produced on the great critic. "One day
I went to visit Belinsky, just before dinner, and as
I crossed the court-yard of his house saw him
sitting by the window of his study with a bulky
manuscript in his hand, and was not a little surprised at the excited way in which he beckoned to
me and began crying out, "Make haste and come
here, I have a rare piece of news for you!" And
scarcely had I entered the room before he ex
claimed, holding out the manuscript to me : "For
two whole days I have been unable to tear myself
away from it. It is a novel by a new writer,—
who or what he is I do not know; but he has
revealed to me traits and characters in Russian
life which none of us have had the wit to discover. You understand, this is the first attempt

that has ever been made by a Russian to write a socialistic novel; and, as is nearly always the case with a true genius, the author all the while evidently has had no idea of what he really was doing."

No one who has read the tale will care to dispute the justice of Belinsky's verdict; and yet, how simple is the story it relates; how natural and unbookish its language; how commonplace and trivial its incidents; how socially insignificant its characters. It introduces us to that numerous class of "trodden-down toilers," as the novelist names them, who think they are rich and lucky if they can hire a whole room for themselves and family, and are oftener obliged to put up with what the Russians call "a clean corner,"—that is, a small portion of a room, partitioned off with a high screen. In such a corner lived Dayvouschkin, a poor *tchinovnik*, whose one difficulty in life was, with his scanty earnings, to keep his brass-buttoned uniform and boots in sufficiently decent order so as not to attract the attention of "his excellency," the chief of the department in which he served. But poor as he was, and though not seldom it necessitated his denying himself a dinner for a day or so, he was never so poor but he could buy for Barbara, his cousin, who lodged

in a bare ill-furnished room on the opposite side
of the court-yard of the house in which he lived,
stuff to make curtains for her window, some little
cheap ornament for her dress, or a few pots of her
favourite flowers wherewith to make her room
·more homelike.   And if at times a feeling of
envious discontent at the wealth of others came
over him, it was rather for her sake than his own
that he lamented his poverty, though even then
he would quickly chase away such thoughts as
impious murmurings against God's will.   "Each
of us," he writes in a letter to her, "has his lot in
life ordained by One who knows better than we
can what is good for us.   One man is destined to
be a general and to wear epaulettes ; another to
be a titular counsellor ; some are born to command, others to obey."   And this spirit of submission, however strange and unreasonable it may
appear to some of us, was based on a deep religious sentiment that formed the guiding principle
of his every act.   In his simple creed, a good
deed loses all worth the instant it is performed
with the anticipation or hope of reward ; and so
thoroughly does he carry out his rule of self-
·effacement, that he forbears expressing to Barbara,
or acknowledging to himself, the nature of the
love he feels for her lest his kindly care for

her comfort and welfare should ever appear to be tainted with self-seeking.

The novelist, it need scarcely be said, does not pretend that all poor *tchinovniks* are like Day-vouschkin, and we may admit that he is a rare exception without in any way diminishing the force of the lesson which the story is evidently designed to teach. The possibility of his existence shows us that, even in natures the most crushed and humiliated, the presence of the heavenly, common to us all, may be found. However dull and joyless their life may be, the human heart still beats in it and sympathisingly responds to the joys and griefs of others.

And if this be true of Dayvouschkin, it is equally true of men like old Petrovsky, the father of the poor student who dies of consumption. There is nothing heroic in the cheated husband of a worthless woman, and we smile at his blind affection for his son, reminding us of the love a dog has to his master; but in spite of his drunkenness and queer follies, the story of his life touches and moves us. Indeed, it would not be easy to name any scene in Russian fiction in which humour and pathos are so powerfully combined as in the description of the burial of the student.

"Anna Fedorovna, the landlady, undertook all arrangements concerning the funeral. A very plain, ready-made coffin was bought, and a carter's truck was hired. To cover any expenses she might have to incur, she at once took possession of the books and few chattels belonging to the deceased. The old man disputed and fought with her about the books, carried off as many as he could, stuffing his pockets full with them, cramming two or three into his hat, and would not part with them for an instant, but took them with him, even into the church. All those three days he was, as it were, dazed and out of his mind, and with restless, anxious disquietude was each moment altering and arraying the solitary wreath on the coffin, or lighting, extinguishing, and changing the wax tapers that were burning before it. It was plain that he could not fix his mind on anything, or bring his thoughts into order. Neither mother nor Anna Fedorovna went to the church; mother was too ill to stir out, and Anna Fedorovna, after she was ready and dressed, got into a hot quarrel with the old man, and shut herself up in the room. So he and I were the only people there. During the whole of the service I was possessed with a strange, mysterious dread, and my soul was filled with a terrible pre-

sentiment of some impending sorrow. At last
the coffin was screwed down, hoisted on to the
truck, and we set off. I accompanied it as far as
the corner of the street. The carter started at a
good smart pace. The old man ran behind, sob-
bing and weeping aloud, his quivering voice keeping time with his quick, uneven steps. The wind
caught his hat, and it fell off, but he did not stay
to pick it up. His bare head was soon drenched
with the rain, and the drizzling sleet dashed against
his shrivelled face; but he did not seem to feel
the sharp weather, and trotted on, running from
one side to the other of the truck. The flaps of
his old torn coat fluttered in the breeze, and stood
out like wings behind him. Books were sticking
out of each of his pockets, whilst in his hands he
held tightly a huge old volume. The people, as
they passed by, took off their hats and crossed
themselves; some stopped a minute to stare with
astonishment at the poor old man. More than
once a volume fell out of his pockets into the
mud, and some one in the street would cry out to
him, and he would hurriedly pick it up, try to rub
it dry with the wet dirty cuffs of his coat, and then
run on quickly to catch up the cart. At the farther
end of the street a beggar-woman joined the old
man, and together with him followed the coffin;

and then they turned round the corner, and were lost to sight, and I made my way back home."

In one of his novels, "The Injured and Insulted," Dostoevsky has described his experiences during the first years of his literary career. "You are a mere writing machine," Natasha exclaims to the hero; "there is nothing spontaneous in your work; you are expected to turn out so much material within an allotted time; you force your thoughts, and thus both body and mind are injured. Look at C——, he will take two years to write a tale, and N—— is occupied ten years on one novel, and for that reason their work is free from blemishes, the result of carelessness and haste." "They can afford to do it," he answers with bitterness; "they are in no anxiety about to-morrow's bread; whilst I,—well, I am a literary hack." His extremely straitened circumstances compelled Dostoevsky to write for money rather than for fame, and he was only too glad to abandon his idea of composing a regular, well-thought-out romance, and to accept the offer made him by Kraevsky, and became a constant contributor to the "Annals of the Country," in which he published from month to month a number of short and hurriedly-written tales and sketches. Many a time he received money in advance for a story he had not even begun, and then had to write day and night, constantly haunted by the dread lest he should fail to have it ready by the promised date. The strain was too great for a constitution never very robust, and the excessive labours of these years, coupled with all the worry and annoyances inseparable from a hand-to-mouth life, first brought on those epileptic fits from which he henceforth suffered till the day of his death.

Several of the tales he wrote at this period acquire an additional interest from the connexion they have with his own sorrows, privations, and disappointments. Thus the fate of the hero of " A Faint Heart " ceases to strike us as exaggeratedly sentimental when we remember that the novelist, with his irritable nervous temperament, himself endured and went through sufferings scarcely less torturing than those which brought poor Schoumkoff to end his days in a lunatic asylum. Madly in love with his young bride, he spends whole days in her society, and quite forgets he has to make a fair copy of certain voluminous official papers, which must be given in by the end of the year. When at last he sets to work, it is too late ; there is no possibility of finishing in time ; and he is terrified at the idea that his failure may involve his being drafted into the

G

army as a common soldier,—the usual punishment in those cruel days for offences of the most trifling kind. Evening after evening he writes and writes in the vain hope of getting through his task, till one night his friend, who shares the same room with him, to his horror remarks that Schoümkoff is scribbling away with a dry pen, turning over one page after another with feverish impatience, and throwing aside, as if they were finished, sheets of paper on which not a word had in reality been written. And, as he watched the poor crazed *tchinovink*, strange thoughts, we are told, came into his mind. For the first time he understood what the agony and fear were that possessed and shattered his friend's soul and reason. "His lips trembled, his eyes gleamed with a strange light, his whole face grew pale, and a new sight, as it were, was granted him, revealing to him in that minute something he had never known or grasped before."

What, then, is the lesson, new to many of us, which, together with his friend and biographer, we may learn, as we read the story of Schoumkoff's life, and listen to the madman's piteous cry : " In what is she to blame, and why must she suffer for my fault?" The earlier years of Dostoevsky's literary career were dogged with poverty and physical sufferings that robbed his life of all joy and made his days a burden and a curse. Those with whom he mixed were, for the most part, like himself,—men who, from the contrast between their social and intellectual position, could not but be struck with the inequalities of life and the crying injustices that reigned around them,—men whose souls were filled with a bitterness and discontent, it may be morbid, but felt all the more strongly because they dared not express it openly. "There are," he writes in his story entitled "Sleepless Nights," "a number of queer, strange corners in St. Petersburg, places into which the sun that warms and cheers its other inhabitants seldom or never penetrates, but which are dimly lighted by a different sun,—a sun we might suppose to have been especially created for these spots, into which it shines with a dull, peculiar light. In these corners men and women live a life quite different to that which surges around us,—a life we might expect to find in some remote, far-off planet, but not in our days and in our immediate neighbourhood. For this life is a medley of the fantastic and the ideal, and at the same time so piteously prosaic and common, not to say so impossibly mean and base." It is this life that Dostoevsky knew and has described. Nor was he able, like some of his

contemporaries, to content himself with finding an
artistic pleasure in sketching its distinguishing
feature, but what he saw he felt and brooded
over.

A strong impulse was given to the feeling of
discontent, which at that time, owing to the stern
rule of a Nicholas, generally obtained among the
cultured and student classes of Russia by the revolutionary movement then agitating France and
the whole of Western Europe. The works of St.
Simon, Fourier, and Leroux, despite censorial
prohibitions, were read with avidity, and secret
societies founded for the purpose of propagating
their ideas and carrying them into active practice.
At the head of one of these societies was a certain
Petraschevsky, an old pupil of the Alexander
Lyceum, and with whom Dostoevsky was slightly
acquainted. He attended some of its meetings,
and took part in more than one of its weekly discussions. If we may judge from the official reports,
these debates mainly turned on abstract questions,
and to an Englishman, accustomed from his youth
to freedom of speech, must seem to have been
singularly harmless and inoffensive. It is true that
at times, as we might expect, the young disputants
would wax warm and give utterance to the most
violent and revolutionary ideas. Thus, on one

occasion Dostoevsky, in the course of a speech, defended the thesis that the Russian people would never follow in the steps of the French revolutionists, and proceeded to quote the well-known lines by Poushkin :—

" Shall I live, dear friends, to see the people unoppressed,
And slavery, by the will of our Tsar, disappear from the land ;
And will the dawn of fair liberty break at length,
And spread over our native land its healing rays of light ? "

His remarks were interrupted by one of the members, who declared that it was folly to expect that the emancipation of the peasants could be obtained by legal means, to which Dostoévsky rejoined that he for one honestly believed that the great reform should be effected peacefully and lawfully. But when further pressed with the question : " Well, suppose they cannot be freed without a revolution, what then ? " he passionately cried out : " What then ? why, let us have a revolution ! " Such utterances, however, do not fairly interpret his real opinions. Then, as throughout his life, he was strongly opposed to the introduction into Russia of political schemes of reform based on ideas radically at variance with the traditions of Russian life ; and in the Russian commune, workmen's associations, and co-operative societies discovered a more lasting and normal foundation for future reforms than he could find in the wild, unpractical dreams of French theorists. Nor did he once allow the free opinions adopted by the majority of his associates to shake his belief in the religious creed of the Russian people. " It was easier for me, perhaps, than for any of the others," he tells us in his " Diary of a Writer," " to keep true to the religion of the people, to learn their faith and thoughts, to be one in spirit with their life. I was brought up in a family at once thoroughly Russian and thoroughly religious. From our first childhood we were made familiar with the Gospel, and before my tenth year I knew all the principal episodes in the history of Russia, as related by Karamsin, whose work father used to read to us of an evening."

As always happens, the longer these secret societies existed the theories they advocated grew in extravagance, and the more violent became the policy they proposed to adopt. A noisy dinner in memory of Fourier, at which Petraschevsky wound up his speech by declaring that it was time to put into execution the death-sentence they had pronounced on the Government and on society, was followed a few days later by the arrest of thirty-four of its members, Dostoevsky among the number; though, it should be remarked, he was not present at the banquet. After a short preliminary examination, held at the Department of the Secret Police, they were lodged in the fortress, where they lay for no less than eight months before they were brought to trial. From the letters and memoirs of Speschnieff, Debout, Duroff, and others, which have been published within the last few years, we learn that during their long confinement they were treated by the authorities with a consideration and kindness not always extended to political prisoners. They were allowed to communicate with their friends ; books and writing materials were placed at their disposal ; and it was whilst in prison that Dostoevsky wrote his story, " A Little Hero." A special commission, under the presidency of General Perovsky, was appointed to investigate the affair ; and, if we may credit the testimony of Yastrgzemscky, one of the accused and formerly an inspector in the Technologial Institute, the result of their deliberations was a verdict of not proven ; but, by imperial orders, the case was referred to a higher court for final decision. On the 22nd of December, 1849, the sentence of the court, condemning all the accused to death, was formally communicated to the prisoners, and early the same morning they were conveyed in prison vans to Simonovsky Place, and there made to stand in three lines on a large scaffold. The terrible sentence was read aloud by one of the court-auditors, and, during the reading, Dostoevsky turned to Duroff, who stood next to him, and whispered: "It cannot be that they will shoot us!" Duroff made no reply, but pointed to a large cart, drawn up close to the scaffold, and on which were strapped a number of plain wooden coffins, partially covered with mat-packing. A priest then stepped forward, bearing a cross, and invited them to confess; but, though all bent down and reverently kissed the cross, only one of them,—Schaposchnikoff,—left the ranks in response to the priest's call. The condemned had now lost all hope that the sentence would not be carried out, and silently prepared themselves to meet their fate with what calmness they could. But one of them,—Kaschkin,—a young Government clerk, who had not yet completed his nineteenth year, was struck with the strange fact that, though he had confessed, Schaposchnikoff was not allowed to receive the Sacrament. He happened to be placed at the extreme corner of the platform, and, availing himself of his position, leaned down to where Galachoff, the Policemaster, was standing, and hurriedly asked him in French : " Is it possible that the priest can hear our confession, and at the same time refuse us the Sacrament?" "Mais vous serez tous pardonnés," the General whispered in reply. In the meantime, the hideous formalities of the law were duly gone through. "We stood on the scaffold," Dostoevsky relates in the "Diary of a Writer," "and listened to the sentence read out to us without the slightest feeling of repentance or regret. Of course, I have no right to speak for the rest, but I believe I am justified in saying that, if not all, the greater number of us would, even in that awful moment, have felt it a disgrace to have recanted any one of our opinions. During those last ten minutes of life, as we stood face to face with death, some of us, as I know on the surest evidence, instinctively searched into our souls, and, it may be, in that short interval of time had taken account of the few years of our young lives, and repented those acts of wrong and ill from which no man is wholly free. But with reference to the special act for which we were condemned and must so soon suffer, the thoughts and convictions of our mind : this seemed to us not only to demand no repentance, but rather to be something that purified and raised the soul, to die for which might justly win pardon for our many faults and short-comings." At the command of the superior officer, three of them,—Petraschevsky, Mombell, and Grigorieff,—were led out and bound to separate posts, and in front of each, at the distance of a few feet a small company of soldiers was drawn up. The soldiers had been ordered to make ready, and the guns were levelled, when the chief officer waved a handkerchief, and the prisoners, were informed that, by the will of the Emperor, the extreme penalty of the law would be remitted. But when, in his turn, Grigorieff was unlashed from his post, he burst into a flood of passionate tears, uttered a wild, incoherent cry, and was carried from the square a raving madman.

Dostoevsky's sentence was commuted to penal servitude in Siberia for four years, with, at the expiration of that period, enforced military service in the ranks for the rest of his life. On Christmas Eve of the same year, his brother was informed that, together with Duroff, he would late that night commence the first stage of his long and tedious journey to Omsk. With some little difficulty he obtained permission to see him once more before his departure, and, in company with a mutual friend,—M. Mieloukoff,—arrived at the Fortress punctually at the hour that had been appointed them. "We were shown into a large room," writes the friend, "in the lower story of the Command-

ant's house. The evening was already far advanced,
and the room was dimly lighted by a single lamp.
We had to wait a considerable time, and twice we
heard the chimes of the Fortress church ring the
quarters. At length the door opened, the thud
of a gun's butt-end sounded sharply on the stone
floor, and Dostoevsky and Duroff, closely followed
by an officer, stood before us. We silently exchanged a warm shake of the hands. Notwithstanding their eight months' confinement, we could
detect but little change in their looks ; the one
still preserved his serious, thoughtful expression,
whilst the face of the other was lighted up with its
wonted childish smile. They were both dressed
in the convict's long travelling cloak, in short fur
overcoats, and in high, felt boots. The officer on
duty courteously drew his chair as far away from
us as he could, and left us to converse freely with
one another. Dostoevsky began by telling his
brother how glad he was that he had escaped their
fate, and then put a number of questions concerning
the health and well-being of his family and children.
But what most struck me in this farewell interview
between the two brothers was, that the one who
was to remain behind in Petersburg seemed to feel
the parting the more acutely. Tears filled his eyes
each time he spoke, and his lips trembled with

the emotion he tried in vain to suppress, whilst
Dostoevsky remained outwardly calm, and was
mainly eager to tranquillise him.   'And even in
the galleys I shall find, not wild beasts, but men,
and, it may be, men better and worthier than I
am. We shall see one another again, I hope.
Hope ! nay, I am sure we shall. And you will
write to me, yes ! And when I have got a little
settled send me some books : I will let you have
a list ; for I shall be allowed to have books there.'
In saying this he probably only wished to cheer
the brother a little.   'And when I leave the galleys, you know, I will begin to write again. These
months I have learned a great deal ; out there I
shall learn still more what life really is, and I shall
have something to write about.' The interview
lasted a little more than half an hour, and, before we
could realise how quickly the time had passed, the
officer reminded us that, according to the rules,
we could not remain any longer. For the last time
we kissed each other, and then with a long, silent
grasp of the hand they tore themselves away, and
we were alone. Having been told that they would
set off in less than an hour, we waited under the
outer gate of the Fortress. It was a cold, bright
night. The chimes had just struck nine when two
sledges drove up, and the prisoners, guarded by

two gendarmes, took their places. ' Farewell ! ' we cried out to them. ' To our next meeting ! ' was the reply, as they drove quickly off."

From the few letters written to his brother during his long exile we can form some idea of what the sufferings were he was called on to endure, and the spirit in which he supported them. It was only after he had quitted the galleys that he was allowed to hold any communication with the outer world. "Already ten months have passed," he writes in a letter dated November 6, 1854, "since I left the mines and began my new life. All those four years I was like a man buried alive, nailed down in his coffin. How awful they were no human pen can describe. They were one unbroken round of inexpressible, endless woe, and each hour, each minute weighed and crushed my soul like some heavy paving-stone. For four whole years I never breathed or moved, never made the shortest step without feeling that I was at the galleys. But why try to explain ? If I were to fill up a hundred sheets of paper you would still have no idea of what my life really was. To understand that you must have seen with your own eyes, or rather have experienced it yourself." And, when he had served his time as convict, the indignities to which he was subjected, particularly during the five years

he was quartered as a common soldier at Semipa-
latinsk, were, if possible, harder to endure than all
he had gone through at the galleys. "God send
you peace and happiness," he writes in 1856,
"and may you never know the horrors that fall to
the lot of some among us: I speak from experience. Everything is against me, and I am in
despair. It is not easy to suffer what I have suffered. I cannot tell all; I am alone, and must
remain alone, in my helpless agony." Cut off from
all he cared for, debarred every pursuit that could
interest, condemned to the most humiliating
drudgeries, his health shattered and ruined by
daily deprivations,—moneyless, homeless, and
friendless,—what wonder if there were moments
when he lost all hope and prayed for death?
After long waiting and repeated disappointments
he obtained permission to resume his literary
career. In 1858 he was raised, chiefly through the
intercession of his old schoolfellow, General
Todleben, to the rank of under-officer; and in the
following year, on the accession of Alexander II.,
was at length recalled from exile. Whilst an officer
he married Madame Isaieff, a widow lady, who, however, died two years after his return to Petersburg.

When we have read the story of Dostoevsky's
life in Siberia, so far as he has thought fit to relate

it, and seen how, in spite of long and cruel suffering, he returned with an unbroken and loyal faith
in the religious and political institutions of his
country, we can easily understand the love,—I
had almost said idolatry,—in which his name is
held by every Russian. A weaker man would have
come back embittered and eager to make war
on society. M. Aksakoff has told us that once
Dostoevsky, together with Mackenzie Wallace and
others, was spending the evening with him, when
the conversation turned on the character of the
Emperor Nicholas, of whom the novelist spoke in
terms of the highest praise. After his departure,
the Englishman came up to Aksakoff, and asked,—

" Did you tell me that was Dostoevsky ? "

" Yes."

" The author of ' Memorials of the House of
Death ' ? "

" The same."

" But it cannot be he who was exiled to the
mines ? "

" No other ; and pray why not ? "

" Why, how could he eulogise the very man who
sent him to the galleys ? "

" You, as a foreigner," replied Aksakoff, " may
find it difficult to understand, but to us it is intelligible, and is thoroughly Russian."

I may remark that Count Tolstoi, who better than any other knows the true character of the Russian people, has brought out this national trait in the scene in his story, " By what Rule Men should Live," where the stranger says to Simon, the shoemaker : " No one has done me wrong : it is God who punishes." And the simple peasant, unversed in the disputes of creeds, is satisfied, and, without a demur, acknowledges : " Of course ; we know all comes from God." It was in this spirit that Dostoevsky bore and endured, found good in what seemed to be evil, and learned the true uses of adversity. " No, it was just," he on one occasion remonstrated to a friend who had been denouncing his exile as wrongful and un-righteous; " the Russian people would have con-demned us. That I only learned there in the galleys. And, besides, who knows but that, in thus punishing me, it was God's purpose to teach me the one thing needful, without which man cannot live, and which can be found alone among the people,—criminals, thieves, murderers, drunk-ards though they be,—and that, in my turn, I should teach it to others, so that they,—not all, only a few,—should become a little better, accept the truth, however partially, and finally be led to escape the abyss into which they are falling."

But whilst, like Tolstoi, it is to the people that Dostoevsky makes his final appeal, there is, in the enunciation of the truth he would have us learn from them, a tone of vague mysticism that, to a large extent, deprives his teaching of that practical bearing without which the loftiest and purest creed will be barren and profitless. He believed that it is reserved for the Russian people to form a social state, the binding principle of which shall be no external contract or forced obligation, but love to one's neighbour; in other words, to realise the high ideal of the Gospel, and replace the arbitrary formal ties that now unite society by the higher spiritual bond of charity and love. No one will dispute that, theoretically, it is the ideal after which, whether orthodox Russians or not, we ought all to strive. Hitherto, at least, Russian progress has not been guided by any such lofty law, and we may reasonably doubt whether it ever will be the recognised and leading principle of national development in Russia or elsewhere. It is a good thing to aspire, but our aspirations, to be of any practical worth, should be accompanied with the modest consciousness that they are but pious wishes, the full completion of which can never be attained, unless, indeed, the conditions of human nature become radically changed, and men be no longer actuated by selfish and utilitarian motives.   Nor can we forget that Alexis and Zozime, the two types of this ideal, are not brought into close contact with the strife and battle of actual life, and, though Dostoevsky intended to represent them in this relation, in the concluding portion of his last unfinished novel, "The Karamazoff Family," we may, without fear of erring, presume that their portraits would have been sketched with far less similitude to reality than the imperfect and erring heroes he has elsewhere drawn for us from his own personal observation and experience.

But if we regard these idealised portraits as potential, rather than actual types, we need not, therefore, be blind to the thoroughly human point of view from which Dostoevsky ordinarily sketches his characters.   In all his novels, beginning with "Poor People," and ending with "The Karamazoff Family," the fundamental motive of his characterisation is the capacity common to all his personages, however low, fallen, and degraded they may be, to experience in a moment of ecstatic enthusiasm, called forth by some rare and exceptional circumstance in their lives, an irresistible excitement to an act of the highest self-devotion and self-denial.   It is in these moments that the spark of human feeling, seemingly stifled in them by the noxious poison of worldliness they have so long breathed, bursts forth with strength sufficient to enable them to overcome and rise above those lower instincts of their nature to which they are habitually enslaved. In this they are like the heroes of Tourgenieff's novels, but here the resemblance ends. For whilst these, when the moment of enthusiasm has passed, sink into despair and fall back into the state of pessimistic unbelief from which they were for an instant stirred, Dostoevsky's heroes zealously guard the remembrance of the victory gained as their brightest and most precious possession, the memory of which brightens up and gladdens their darkest and gloomiest days. And as we read the story of their lives we are made to share this feeling. The manifestations of spiritual strength in these outcasts of our race inspire us with a belief in the possibility of a higher and more perfect happiness for mankind, and encourage us in the desire to work with and for those who, now crushed by poverty, ignorance, and neglect, have still within them the seed of life that requires but warmth and kindly culture to bring forth the richest and ripest of fruit. It is in this faith that Dostoevsky lived and wrote, and in all his works he speaks the word of love and trust to the suffering and oppressed classes of his countrymen. None, save those who have finally and entirely lost all hope and belief, can for an instant doubt that the call will be heard and responded to.

In the second year after his return from Siberia, Dostoevsky published his novel, "The Injured and Insulted." Its faults of construction are numerous and glaring; the plot, in itself improbable, is inconsistently worked out; the blind, unreasoning love of Natasha for the empty-headed chatterer, Alexis, is irritatingly unnatural; the character of the wicked prince is drawn too melodramatically; and the personages habitually talk in a language appropriate to the author, but altogether out of harmony with their temperament and position. And yet, in spite of all these shortcomings, we read the novel with interest and avidity. "I know," writes Dostoevsky, in a letter to his brother, "what I wished to produce, but a rough, wild piece of work is all I have succeeded in turning out, though there are some fifty pages or so of which I am proud." Among the fifty pages to which he refers with such pride must be included those dedicated to the story of little Nellie. From her childhood she had been the witness and victim of wrong and injustice. In the long hours she passed by the bedside of her dying mother, cast off and abandoned to poverty by the man for whom she had gladly made the dearest sacrifices, refused pardon and forgiveness by the husband she had betrayed, Nellie, whilst yet a child, was made to feel the unpitying selfishness of the world, and the indiscriminating sternness of its moral law. She has thus learned to distrust, and will not remain under obligation even to the man who rescues her from the hands of a Boubnova, and thus saves her from a life of shame and dishonour. But she never loses her faith in mankind, though she looks with suspicion and doubt on individuals. "There is no shame in begging," she declares, when Ivan Petrovitch finds her in the streets soliciting alms that she may have wherewith to buy necessaries for her mother; " I do not beg of any one man, I beg of all, and all are not one man : it were a shame to ask charity of one, but there is no disgrace in asking alms of all." Little by little he wins her confidence, and, with the impulsiveness of a simple, unspoiled nature, she devotes herself to him heart and soul, and cannot bear that he should give a thought or care to others. She is jealous of Natasha, in whose fate he is so warmly interested, and, rather than share what she believes to be a divided affection, is ready to return to the life from which he had taken her. But when she learns the story of Natasha's mad love for Alexis, and how her father had cursed her and banished her from his presence, her heart goes out towards her, and she gladly aids him in bringing about a reconciliation between father and daughter. She tells him of her mother; how she too had been driven from home, with a father's curse still ringing in her ears, and how, when at last he came with the tardy message of peace, he found her dead, deaf to all human pity or blame, already in the presence of One who judges with larger, other eyes than ours. The old man is touched, and ere it is too late forgives his erring child. The whole life of Nellie is thus a protest against human justice. When, soon after, she herself is dying, she calls Ivan Petrovitch to her bedside, and bids him : "Go to him, and tell him I died without forgiving him. Tell him I have this very morning been reading my Bible, but I do not forgive him, because when mother was dying, and could hardly speak, her last words were, 'I curse him.' And so now I, her daughter, curse him, not for any harm he has done me, but for the sin he did her." After her death, a little bag that hung from her neck is opened, and found to contain a letter written by her mother to the prince who had betrayed her, in which she tells him that in heaven she will pray for him, and learn to forgive, if only he will care for and be kind to little Nellie, her child and his daughter. That letter had never been given to the prince, nor did she once try to bring him to account. Human law, had she appealed to its protection, would doubtless have compelled him to fulfil the dying woman's prayer, but in the eyes of Nellie no earthly court could redeem the offence and insult. She, therefore, sought no redress, and it was to a higher tribunal that she carried her complaint.

No analysis can possibly give an adequate idea of the charm the novelist has thrown over this episode in his romance. Of equal merit are the scenes in which the life of Natasha's family, the Ichmeneffs, is described. Readers who, like Partridge at the play, admire loud speaking and noisy rant, will, of course, find them dull and insipid; but all who have an ear for the true and simple, must acknowledge their exceptional worth. The hero, Ivan Petrovitch, who had lived with them in their more prosperous days, one evening brings to them the manuscript of his first novel; and the old man, Nicholas Sergeivitch, together with his wife, Anna Andreevna, and

Natasha, form the young author's first public
audience :—

"I read to them my romance in one sitting.
We began directly after tea, and the reading continued till two o'clock in the early morning. At
first, the old man was evidently put out. He
had expected something immeasurably grander,
something that, in all probability, he would not
have understood, but, all the same, something
undoubtedly magnificent and lofty. And, instead
of that, a poor lot of ordinary people, and the
most common events, exactly such as they themselves had experienced a thousand times. If the
hero had only been a great man, an interesting
character, an historical celebrity, like Roslavlieff,
or Youric Miloslavsky ! But to make a hero of a
little, miserable, stupid *tchinovnik*, the buttons on
whose uniform were greasy and torn,—and all
described in language neither better nor worse
than we ourselves employ,—that could not be
right. The old woman looked inquisitively at her
husband, and seemed to feel that she had been
cheated, and was accordingly offended.

"'Is it worth while to print and read such
rubbish ?' she appeared to be saying to herself.
'And to think he will get paid for it !'

"Natasha was all attention, listened greedily,

did not once take her eyes off me, as she watched each movement of my lips, whilst hers moved in response, as though she were mentally repeating each word. And what do you think? Before I had half finished, tears filled the eyes of all my listeners. Anna Andreevna wept outright, and I understood, from her naïve explanations, how, with all her heart, she only wished that she could help my poor hero in his struggles and misfortunes.

" ' It is not from the first step,' Nicholas Sergeivitch said, 'that the end of a long journey is to be seen. And so it is with us. At first, we think, a mere story-teller ; then, the heart is touched ; little by little all that is happening gets intelligible and interesting ; and, at last, we are made to comprehend and feel that the veriest outcast, the last and lowest of men, is one with ourselves and a brother ! '

" Natash listened and wept, as, under the table, she silently but warmly pressed my hand. The reading was finished. She rose hurriedly, her cheeks all on fire, and her eyes overflowing with tears. Suddenly she seized my hand, kissed it, and rushed from the room. Her father and mother exchanged looks of puzzled bewilderment.

" ' Ah well, she was always of an excitable

temper,' the old man muttered; 'but there is no harm in that. It is a good feeling. Yes, she is a brave, noble girl.'

" ' Well,' exclaimed his wife, ' of course Alexander of Macedonia is a hero; but that is no reason for beginning to break the chairs and furniture.' "

LECTURE IV.

Theodore Michaelovitch Dostoevsky.

Part II.

Few who have travelled in the north-eastern districts of Russia can fail to have met from time· to time bands of people in grey jackets and cloaks, with closely-shaven heads, and heavy irons .clamped round their ankles, wearied and way-worn, as they drag themselves along the rough, uneven road. They are prisoners, or, as the Russians like to call them, " unfortunates," on their way to the Siberian galleys. The passer-by will stop a few minutes, cross himself, distribute his charity among them, and then hurry on. In his eyes they are but a crowd of criminals, murderers, and thieves. We have all read of their sufferings in prison, and of the still harder fate of those who have to work in the mines. But till Dostoevsky wrote his " Memorials of the House of Death," our only sources of information as to the life of these Siberian convicts were either dry, incomplete official records, or the narrative of some traveller who could only tell the very little he was allowed by the authorities to see and inspect. He first introduced us to this new world, a country of woe and suffering, so intense and so crushing that few who have once crossed its borders have had strength to survive the miseries they there endured. The perusal of his book produces on us an impression not less profound and harrowing than Dante's pictures of Hell; only these are no fantastic regions, the creation of a poet's imagination, but real and actual. There is not a single crime that does not find its representative here, and, huddled together in one common barrack, the born criminal, the murderer by profession, the innocent dupe, the half-mad fanatic, the honest political enthusiast, are one and all subjected to the same stern punishment, and have to suffer the same death in life. For four years Dostoevsky lived with these men, the air filled day and night with brutal oaths, coarse jokes, rude quarrels, and drunken orgies. We may wonder how, brought up as he had been, he could have supported such an existence; but, as he reminds us with one of those touches of truthful humour we so often find in his writings, " there is nothing to which a man cannot get accustomed." Besides, in the very worst of them, in the murderer Gazine (who had

enticed a young child into a by-road, and there
hacked him up slowly into pieces, as he watched
with fiendish delight the convulsive twitchings of
his helpless victim), no less than in the venerable
Old Believer, who had committed no offence save
that of remaining true to his faith and creed; or in
the simple, pure-souled Alexis, who passed his
leisure time in reading the Bible, and would hush
all grumbling discontent at their fate with the
assurance that Isaiah was a great prophet : in each
of them he discovered those traits of human
nature which might seem to have been effaced by
the all-destroying power of some outburst of wild
passion, but which still lay dormant in the heart of
the lowest criminal. "It often happens in the
galleys," he writes, "that you have known a man
for years, and have come to regard him as an
animal rather than a human creature, when
suddenly, and in a chance minute, the true soul of
the man unexpectedly reveals itself, and you find
in him feeling, heart, consciousness of his own
vices, and sympathy with the sorrows of others, so
that you can only gaze with wonder, and are
unable for a while to believe the testimony of your
own eyes and ears."

Whilst reading Dostoevsky's work, we must not
forget that, since it was written, many changes

have been made in the criminal law of Russia, and in the administration of her prisons. The peasant is no longer a serf, to be whipped or exiled to Siberia at the will of his owner ; military discipline has lost much of its former harshness ; magisterial courts, with trial by jury, have been established; and, as a natural result of these reforms, the number of offences for which transportation to the mines is the legal penalty has been considerably diminished. But in spite of these concessions to the requirements of a humaner age, the book points out certain evils that are still unreformed, and which strangely clash with the most elementary ideas of right and justice. No distinction, beyond the term of exile to which they are sentenced, is made either in the kind of labour on which the convicts are employed, or in the rigorous nature of the imprisonment to which they are exposed. The consequence is that hardened criminals, and those who have been led into crime through mere thoughtlessness and chance temptation, or are guilty of what in happier times would be regarded as no offence at all, are not only lodged together, but are punished with equal severity. Our moral sense revolts at the idea that political offenders like Dostoevsky or Duroff should be forced to herd with the most depraved of murderers, nor can we by any jugglery be persuaded to regard their venial faults as deserving the punishment meted out to the ruffianly excesses of a Gazine. As we read of the unmerited ignominies they, and many like them, were called on to suffer, and think of the waste of strength involved in their forced exclusion from those spheres of activity wherein they might have worked and laboured for the good of their country, we can only ask, as the author does in the concluding lines of his " Memorials,"—" Who is to blame, and who is really in fault, that all this power has been thus blindly, wilfully, and irreparably thrown away ? "

Dostoevsky's " Crime and Punishment," published in 1866, is almost as direct an outcome of his Siberian experiences as the " Memorials of the House of Death." Characters like Rascolnikoff are, fortunately for us, abnormal and exceptional ; but, among the criminals with whom his lot was cast, Dostoevsky more than once came across men who, naturally kind, generous, and unselfish, had, under the influence of a radically-false theory of life, over which they allowed themselves to brood, been led to commit some foul and brutal crime. A poor student, eager in his search after knowledge, he is hampered and impeded at every step,

and made to feel more sharply than he might
have done, had he been engaged in work
demanding only physical labour and energy, the
inequalities of life, believes the world to be sadly
out of joint, and is convinced that our existing
social order is based on wrong and injustice. But
it is not his own deprivations or the hardships he
has himself to endure, so much as pity for and
sympathy with the poverty and sufferings of
others, that make him the sworn foe of wealth and
rank. Poor though he was, he still contrived, with
the scanty wages he earned by giving lessons, to
support for six months a sick fellow-student, and,
when his friend died, expended his last to secure
for him a fit and decent burial. And his attach-
ment to the daughter of his landlady is chiefly
motived by a feeling of commiseration for her
hard and cheerless lot. "I do not know," he
confesses after her death, "what it was that
attached me to her, unless it were that she always
was ill and ailing. Had she been lame or hump-
backed, in all probability I should have loved her
still more." Some of us may find it difficult to
understand Rascolnikoff's tenderness of heart,
and be disposed to ridicule it as maudlin and
sentimental. But if we remember that he lived
surrounded by abject want and starving poverty,

of which most of us have only read and heard,
we may, perhaps, be able to comprehend how
his heart bled within him as each day and every
hour he witnessed misery he had. no power to
mitigate or relieve. What must have been the
impression produced on such a nature by his visit
to the cold-hearted, grasping usuress, with whom
he pawns for a rouble and a half the last of his
possessions,—the watch his dying father had given
him ! Need we wonder, if, whilst she was beating
him down, and then discounted the heavy interest
from the trifling loan she finally agreed to advance,
the idea came into his head that he would be
doing a righteous deed were he to murder the
greedy hag, rob her of her ill-gained wealth, and
with it help those who, through no fault of their
own, had not the means to feed themselves and
their hungry children.

It is whilst he is in this dangerous state of mind
that Rascolnikoff meets the drunken Marmeladoff
at a common tavern. None who have once read
the novel can ever forget the scene that follows.
With a half-comic, half-tragic solemnity of style
and diction, interrupted with bitter self-reproaches,
Marmeladoff relates the hideous story of his home-
life, and tells of the poor consumptive wife, the
hungry starving children, and the terrible price at

I

which Sophie, the eldest daughter, obtains money
to buy them food :—

"I was lying on the bed . . . well, if you will
have it, in a heavy drunken doze . . . when
suddenly I heard Sophie's voice . . . she is
always very gentle, and her voice is soft and low,
she has light flaxen hair, and a pale thin face.
So I listened, and caught the words: 'How,
Catherine Ivanovna, is it possible you can wish
me to go and sell myself like that? Why, Daria
Fedorovna, since she has become a fallen woman,
has got known to the police, and they have been
three times to the landlady, making inquiries
about her.' 'And who are you,' answered my
wife, 'that you must needs take such wonderful
care of yourself; I did not know you were so
precious!' But you must not blame her, do not
blame her, sir! When she spoke thus, she was
not in her right mind ; she was agitated, ill, and
maddened with the tears of the children, who
were crying out for something to eat ; she did not
mean what she said, but spoke in anger, merely
to vent her spite on Sophie. For Catherine
Ivanovna is like that, and often, when the children
are troublesome and will clamour for bread, she
will begin to punish and beat them. And then I
saw Sophie get up from her seat; it was about

six in the evening, and she drew a kerchief over
her head, and put on her little jacket, and left the
house, and it was not till nine o'clock that she returned. She came into the room, went straight
up to Catherine Ivanovna, and silently threw on
the table before her thirty silver rouble pieces.
She did not say a single word, or even look at any
one of us, but took down from a hook the large
woollen shawl, which was their common property,
pulled it close over her head and face, and threw
herself on to her bed, with her face turned to the
wall, her shoulders and whole body trembling
with the sobs she tried to suppress. . . . And
I continued to lie there as before, still drunk.
. . . And some few minutes later, my good
sir, I saw Catherine Ivanovna, also without
uttering a word, go up to Sophie's bed, fall on her
knees, and begin to kiss her feet ; and there she
remained kneeling, and for a long time refused to
get up, and then at last they both fell asleep,
locked in one another's arms, whilst I . . . I still
lay there drunk and dazed."

As Roscolnikoff listens to his story, and hears
how for five days he has been away from home,
spending in drink his last month's salary, as well
as the money he had stolen from his daughter's
drawer, he learns, for the first time, that far worse

than the physical deprivations which poverty
brings with it is the moral degradation of its
victims, too often the destruction and effacement
of all that is pure and noble in their nature. The
old social problem, the unequal distribution of
wealth, that ever since men began to think has
unhinged and perverted weak minds, presents
itself with renewed force, and to him there is but
one solution. With the riches that are now
hoarded in the money chests of the old usuress
and cheats like her how many a Sophie might be
saved from shame and ruin, how many a life's
burden eased and removed! And, as so often
happens in the real world, two chance circumstances, calculated to confirm him in his idea,
occur at the very moment when his mind unconsciously invites persuasion, and is most disposed to yield to any passing temptation. He
receives a letter from home, informing him that his
sister, Dounya, has accepted a brilliant offer, and
is engaged to a certain Loujine, "whom, of
course," as the mother takes care to add, "the
girl does not love, but who is extremely rich and
apparently a good and honourable man." It is
not, then, only Sophie that barters herself away;
and the sole difference is that she does it from
abject want, and for the sake of obtaining the

'bare necessities of life, whilst these other women sell themselves that they may enjoy unnecessary luxuries and comforts. A few days later, he is sitting in the same tavern where he had encountered Marmeladoff, and accidentally overhears a conversation between a student and a young officer. They are talking of the usuress, and the student relates how she has been heard to express her intention of bequeathing her money to a monastery, probably hoping, by this deed of charity, to purchase a good place in the next world. And he proceeds to argue that, if she were put out of the way, her riches might be the means of rescuing dozens of poor families from want and starvation. It is true that, when the officer laughingly asks him, " Will you, then, undertake to murder the hag ? " he immediately answers, " Certainly not ; it is not my business." These words, however, chiming in, as they do, with the theory over which he has so long been brooding, produce a strong and lasting impression on Rascolnikoff's mind. It may be, the student has nothing to do with punishing the ill-doer ; but suppose it is he, Rascolnikoff, who has been called to the work and chosen by fate to be the avenger of wrong. From that moment there is no more doubt or hesitation ; he feels that he is no longer free to judge or to will; and he returns home like a man condemned to death. The time is past for debating whether the end he has in view be righteous or not ; his whole mind is now concentred on arranging the plan of its execution, and overcoming any obstacles that may stand in his way. When he hears a neighbouring church clock strike seven, the hour at which he knows the usuress will be alone in her lodging, he is only afraid that he may be too late. When he sees that it is impossible to steal the hatchet, with which he is to commit his crime, from the landlady's kitchen without being discovered, he only feels a dull brutal anger at what, for the first moment, seems to be an insurmountable difficulty. When he succeeds in getting a hatchet from the *dvornik's* room and, undetected, conceals it under his overcoat, he only experiences a feeling of relief at the thought that he is fully equipped for the work he has undertaken. So possessed is he with the one idea that he and no other is destined to fulfil the decree of fate, that he loses all power to provide against those little oversights which must, if neglected, lead to his conviction. But this mental exaltation only carries him through the crime, and then abandons him. When he has killed the woman, he does not make that use of the stolen money

which he had reasoned himself into accepting as
a full justification of his act. An inferior novelist,
I think, would have represented him as at once
lavishly expending it in deeds of charity, and
thereby winning an easy opportunity for self-praise.
But though Rascolnikoff has a chance of so doing
when Marmeladoff is run over by a carriage and
killed, it is out of the little monthly sum his
mother sends him that he relieves the most
pressing necessities of the family, nor does he
touch or even count the money he has carried off
with him from the room of the usuress, but hurries
to dig a hole somewhere in the earth and bury it
out of sight.

Punishment follows quickly on his crime.
Little by little his eyes are opened, and he is
forced to acknowledge how false were his pre-
tensions to play the part he had assumed, and
that, not love for the suffering and poor, but self-
conceit, and a vain desire to show himself in will
and courage superior to other men, was the real
motive that had actuated him. "It was not," he
says, "from any wish to help poor mother, that
I killed her; all that is nonsense. It was not
that I might get the means and power of doing
good, but it was something quite different that
urged me on. I wished to know, once and for

all, whether I have that within me, or not, to transgress the ordinary limits and raise myself above the common run of men." This melodramatic trait, the longing to play a grand part, is not lightly thrown off, and accompanies Rascolnikoff in his first essays at repentance. He resolves to confess his crime to Sophie, to be guided by her counsel, for she too has sinned, and will not turn from him with aversion. He therefore seeks her out, and, throwing himself at her feet, exclaims: "It is not before thee I bow myself, but to suffering humanity I pay my homage." These words are evidently designed to produce a powerful effect, but Sophie, with that instinctive avoidance of anything like theatrical show, which is a characteristic trait in Russian women of her class, merely asks: "What have you done, what is it you have done against yourself?" She has read but little, has never, like him, written a university dissertation on the nature of crime, but none the less she, without difficulty, understands that he has sinned against himself far more than against others. But though she condemns, the sentence she pronounces is seasoned with mercy. She takes him by the hand, draws him to herself, throws her arms round his neck, and, looking kindly into his eyes, exclaims: "There is not in the whole world a being to be pitied more than you!" All this is quite different to what he had expected : he had looked for something more imposing, more dramatic; he cannot comprehend the feeling by which she is prompted. "What a strange creature you are, Sophie!" he cries out; "you embrace and kiss me at the very moment I am speaking to you of that; you do not know what you are doing." She makes no direct answer, but, going to her little table, takes up her Bible, and begins to read to him the story of Lazarus of Bethany,—of all the Gospel narratives the one that speaks most home to the heart of the common Russian folk. He listens, and for the first time the spiritual meaning of the stupendous miracle is borne upon him, and he feels what the crime he has committed really is. "It is not the old woman I have murdered, but I have killed myself!" In these words is summed up the whole lesson of the novel. For three days, like Lazarus, he has lain in the grave, cramped and bound, till the moment of awakening arrives, and, hearing the divine call, "Come forth!" he casts off the chains and fetters with which he is shackled, stands on his feet, and is once more able to walk in spiritual freedom.

The simpler but stronger nature triumphs over

Rascolnikoff's deadened and perverted soul. He gives himself up to justice, is tried, and exiled to Siberia for life, whither Sophie follows him. "*Matoushka*, Sophie Simonovna, you are our little mother, always kind and gentle, for you have suffered yourself," are the words with which her hourly services of love and sympathy are acknowledged by the rude, rough convicts, so easily moulded, as Dostoevsky has taught us, by those who approach them as creatures differing from ourselves only in the hardness of their fate, so stubborn and obdurate in the hands of those who think they can reform men with the knout and the Siberian mines.

It is not without reason that the novelist has put into opposition to the weak, erring Rascolnikoff the strong, healthy character of his friend and fellow-student, Razoumiechen. "For nearly two hundred years," he says on one occasion, "we have been unlearning the lesson of work. You are all, to a man, chatterers and fine talkers; you breed melancholy, and sit brooding on it as a hen does on her egg. And your grumbling philosophy is stolen from foreign authors; nor do you once show the least sign of self-made or self-independent life." It is an old complaint that we find in nearly every Russian writer, and, unfortunately, the complaint is as true as it is old. But we must not blame too unreservedly the Rascolnikoffs, if their creed of life be too often soulless, unprofitable, and unproductive. The sophisms which they get from books corrupt and turn their natures awry, simply because the conditions of their life have rendered them peculiarly susceptible to such influences and cut them off from all corrective impressions. It is exclusively from books they get their instruction. The lessons of public life they are not allowed to learn. Practical experience, which would soon clear their brains of fantastic theories, is denied them; and, consequently, Rascolnikoffs are less rare phenomena in Russia than elsewhere.

In "Crime and Punishment" we have the diagnosis of a diseased mind, and in his novel entitled "Evil Spirits" Dostoevsky has given us an analysis of a diseased age, and traced the source and origin of Nihilism, the peculiar malady of our epoch. The least pleasing in subject and treatment of all his novels, it is the one in which he most strikingly exhibits his rare power of analysing sickly characters and compelling the reader to watch and follow with interest each detail of the operation. The evil spirits of which it treats are, as its hero explains to us, the sores, miasmas, and impurities that for generations have fastened on and corrupted Russian life. There is something so bizarre in the ideas, conduct, and speech of its leading characters, that we should be tempted to accuse the author of indulging in caricature, did we not know that the story is founded on fact, and is nothing more than a record of Netchaieff's mad attempt to revolutionise Russia. They live in a world of their own, speak a peculiar jargon, and seem to think that, if only they set at defiance every elementary idea of religion and morality, they have made good their claim to be accepted as liberal and enlightened reformers. But we should err, did we suppose that all who took part in the movement were cheats or ignorant enthusiasts. "It was my object in writing 'Evil Spirits,'" we read in Dostoevsky's "Diary of a Writer," "to explain how men like Netchaieff could in our age and generation obtain adepts and followers. . Is it possible to suppose that all his proselytes, or even the majority of them, were unread ignoramuses? I do not believe all were such; I myself am an old Netchaievist, and have stood on the scaffold under sentence of death; and I assure you that many of my fellow-sufferers were men of high education and culture."

If Nihilism so easily took root in Russia, it could

only be because it found there a convenient soil
for its growth. The secret but persistent opposition of the landed nobility to the emancipation
of their serfs, the chicaneries to which they resorted in order to minimise as far as possible the
benefits conferred on the peasantry by the mea-
sure of 1861, naturally produced a general feeling
of disappointment and discontent at the comparatively small results obtained; and it was on
this feeling of dissatisfied discontent that Nihilist
agitators worked with such sinister success. More
especially they traded on the enthusiasm of the
inexperienced, and many a young student, like
poor Erkel in the novel, was inveigled into com-
mitting atrocious and heartless crimes in the
honest and firm belief that he was thereby aiding
in and hastening the inauguration of a new era of
equal happiness. Slaves to this idea,—everything
else seemed to these Erkels to be accidental and
unimportant,—and constituting, as it did in their
eyes, the one reality, there was no crime they
were not ready to perpetrate, no life they were
not willing to sacrifice, in order to secure its
realisation and triumph. Dostoevsky fully acknowledges the pure and unselfish motives by which
men like Erkel were actuated; but none the less
sternly exposes their powerlessness to do more

than promote a temporary political terror. For, whatever acceptance their teaching may find among those who have been brought up in the ideas of Western European revolutionists, it is radically opposed to the religious and political belief of the Russian people. The Russian peasant, when smarting most cruelly under wrong, never loses his faith in the Tsar, and is convinced that he has only to make his grievances known to him to have them at once redressed. With him loyalty is not so much a feeling as a religion, and no practical reform, however good it may be in itself, can possibly be effected, unless it be based on a recognition of the supreme authority of the Tsar. The necessity of preserving that authority intact is persistently inculcated by Dostoevsky and others, who speak with the authority of men that have lived with the people, and are intimately acquainted with their belief. " We are the faithful servants of the Tsar," he writes in one place, " because we are his children, and his people are not ashamed to call themselves his servants."

Although Dostoevsky, to the last, continued writing romances; like most of his Russian contemporaries, before the end of his career he became more a publicist than a novelist. What he was content to suggest in his earlier compositions, in his latest work, "The Karamazoff Family," which he did not live to complete, he preaches and sets forth in every possible form and from every possible point of view. Its characters fall into two sharply divided groups, the sheep and the goats : the former consisting of monks, nuns, and priests ; the latter, of those who live in the world. They do not talk, but sermonise and deliver elaborate discourses of a mystical style on those social and religious questions in which Dostoevsky himself always took a peculiar interest. The author evidently regarded the plot and construction of his story to be a thing of secondary importance, and adopted the form of a fiction simply because many will read a novel who would turn away with aversion from a tractate or long didactic essay.

By reason of the mystic, exalted style which characterises the greater portion of the novel, it is not altogether easy to seize on or to state in plain, succinct language the fundamental idea, to expound and develop which was presumably the author's main object in writing it. The Karamazoff family consists of Theodore Pavlovitch, his three boys, Demetrius, Ivan, and Alexis, and his illegitimate son, Smerdiakoff. They differ widely in disposition and temperament, but are all possessed, to a high degree, with that wild unrest and impetuous impatience which gives an attractive, but, at the same time, dangerous tendency to the policy of typical modern Russian reformers. Desirous of making up for lost time, these theorists advocated and preached the necessity of adopting at once, and in all their entirety, the most advanced ideas of European civilisation, and seemed to imagine that a constitution after the fashion of England or France could be ordered and transported from abroad with as little trouble as a hamper of English stout or a fresh Parisian suit. Under the influence of the revolutionary movement of 1848, a few rash attempts were made to put these theories into practice. These, of course, were easily and quickly put down by the Government. But the measures of repression resorted to were so exceptionally stern and sharp that they overshot their mark, and the re-establishment of order was more apparent than real. Any expression of dissatisfaction, in however mild a form, was rendered impossible ; but the spirit of discontent, so far from being crushed, was driven underground, where it acquired a secret force and extent that only declared itself when the first concessions were made to the party of progress. Great as were the changes introduced into the social and political life of the country during the earlier years of Alexander the Second's reign,—and these changes were carried out with a rapidity that at times bordered closely on rashness,—because all was not done at once, it seemed to the more ardent minds of young Russia that, in reality, nothing had been accomplished. To educate a people in the hard and slowly-learned lesson of self-rule and independence, to train them in those habits which alone can assure the right use of liberty, it was thought sufficient to open a few schools and to write eloquent panegyrics on the blessings of constitutional government. Instead of building on the strong foundations already laid in the past traditions of the Russian people, hot-brained enthusiasts set themselves to the more attractive task of uprooting and destroying the basis on which alone they could have raised a sure and lasting edifice. We all know the result of the mad crimes to which they had recourse in order to finish their work the more speedily.

Ivan Karamazoff, half positivist half pessimist, belongs to this class of dangerous enthusiasts. In one part of the romance he relates to his brother, Alexis, the scheme of his prose-poem, " The Grand Inquisitor," in which he designed to set forth in the person of the hero his own views on man and the world.   The poem is in the form of a dialogue between the inquisitor and Christ, who is supposed to have come again on to the earth and to have been arrested as a teacher of false and heretical doctrines.   The inquisitor reproaches Christ for having come again into the world, and fears that He will hinder him and his in their work of bringing men to faith and obedience. . He prays Him not to repeat the mistake He made during His first advent, when He gave men liberty to interpret the Scriptures, each in his own way, to believe or not to believe; whereas He should have contented Himself with turning stones into bread, and thus satisfied once and for ever the animal instincts and requirements of man.   He might thus have gained the whole world to His cause, if, instead of preaching love and freedom, He had boldly proclaimed His kingly authority, made good His claim by a series of stupendous miracles, and struck terror into the hearts of men.

In all this Ivan Karamazoff is but echoing, with a blunt frankness we are scarcely accustomed to, the theory that lies at the bases of Nihilistic socialism, and which has been turned to their own selfish ends by more than one of our modern saviours of society.   The doctrine is manifestly the outcome and product of a complete disbelief in the possibility of human happiness, and involves the denial of all progress towards perfection. The only happiness that lies within our grasp, if we are to believe these Karamazoffs, is of a negative kind, and consists in freedom from physical suffering and bodily want. "Man is naturally weak and vile," Ivan's inquisitor declares, "you promise him heavenly bread, that is, love and freedom ; but I repeat again, can that, in the eyes of a weak, corrupt, selfish race, compare for a moment with earthly bread ? And if thousands, or tens of thousands, are tempted to follow you for the sake of this heavenly bread, what is to become of the millions, or tens of millions, who have not the strength to prefer the heavenly to the more satisfying bread of this earth ? " And if Ivan is interested in the fate of these millions, it is but abstractedly. The sufferings of humanity, but never of the individual, arouse his sympathy. "I never could understand," he cynically declares, "how a man can be expected to love his neighbour; it is exactly my neighbour I am unable to love." To relieve the actual misery around him is too humble and vulgar a task, and the sphere of home-life is far too narrow for a reformer who believes it is his mission to set right the universe. He feels that there is something wrong in existing social relations, and, with his impulsive, lawless nature, feeling usurps the place of reason and judgment. If he is to have happiness, it must be here, in this world, or he will none of it ; nor does he believe that any deprivation, however trifling, can be redeemed by the promise of bliss in some distant future world. "Your future heaven," he exclaims, with a savage plainness of speech that has the true Karamazoff ring in it, "has already cost me pretty dear. My pockets will not allow me to pay such a high price. And, therefore, I shall lose no more time, but at once return my ticket of admission. I cannot accept your God, Alexis ; all I can do is to give back politely my entrance-ticket."

With Alexis, on the contrary, this hope in the future, this belief in the higher goal of life, made him hold to the ticket which Ivan, in his childish petulance, was ready to throw away as a cheat that can only take in the ignorant and unwary. The remembrance, the more powerful, perhaps, from its very vagueness, of his mother, who died in his early childhood, and still more the example and wise counsel of the aged monk, Zozime, had kept Alexis pure in the midst of the hideous vice that flaunted itself in the home of the Karama-zoffs. To preserve that purity as far as possible untainted, he withdraws from the world, enters the monastery, and puts himself under the spiritual direction of the good Zozime. But he is also attracted to Zozime,—and in this he exhibits the distinguishing trait common to the Karama-zoffs,—by his fame and by the authority he enjoys among the people. And, if he accepts the monk's teaching, and makes his own the fundamental principle of that teaching,—love to one's neighbour and charity in our judgment of men,—it is mainly because it is Zozime, and not another, whom he will have to serve. He believed as fervently as his brother Ivan in the necessity of the strong man if individuals or societies are to be saved, and would have scorned to be the follower of any prophet who did not exercise power. Like the Grand Inquisitor, he was eager for signs and wonders, and when Zozime died, felt a discon-tented impatience at the ways of Providence, because miracles were not wrought at his tomb, and the vouch of supernatural testimony was not given to his mission.

Many of Dostoevsky's readers have found it difficult to understand the sympathetic partiality with which the person of Zozime is drawn, and to his foreign critics in particular the character of the monk and the novelist's enthusiastic eulogy of

monastic life have proved a serious stumbling-
block and a stone of offence. "The monastery,"
he declares, "has been from days immemorial and
in all times Russia's salvation." We all know
Milton's opinion of "cloistered virtue," and most
of us, I presume, are disposed to prefer the bold
wrestler who, "not without dust and heat," strives
to win the prize, to the cautious seeker of salvation that screens himself in monastic retirement
from the wounds and perils of combat. But they
err who would lay down a fast and fixed law for
all men, and the story of the old monk's life, as
related by Alexis, his loving disciple, may well
serve to teach us that the ways of God are many
and diverse.

Originally destined to serve in the army, he
was educated in a military college, and from an
early age accepted as his guide and rule the false ·
ideas of truth and honour which are always inculcated in these establishments. "When we left
with the rank of officers," he confesses, "we were
ready to wipe out with our blood any insult to the
honour of our regiment, though not one of us had
the least idea wherein true honour consists." For
a while he found satisfaction in the pleasures of
the world, and, under the idea of avenging his
honour, on one occasion challenged the husband

of a young girl for no other reason than that he
imagined his claims to her affection to be superior
to those of his rival. This duel formed the
turning-point in his life. For the first time, his
conscience speaks with a voice that no juggling
sophistry can hush, the true nature of the crime
he is about to commit under the specious name
of honour confronts him, and, after his opponent
has shot, he not only fires in the air, but implores
pardon for the wrong of which he himself had
been guilty, and for the sin into which he had
led his antagonist by tempting him to seek the
life of a fellow-creature. As we might expect, his
true motives are misunderstood, and his act forms
the theme of many a sharp epigram and idle
witticism ; but his simple answer, " Yesterday I
was a fool, but to-day I have become wiser," and
his declaration that he has resolved to enter a
monastery, disarm his mockers, and they themselves acknowledge, " It is not for us to judge a
man of God."

But if Zozime himself withdrew from the world,
and believed the work and teaching of the monastery to be the surest means of salvation for the
Russian people, he in no wise advocated a life of
religious idleness, or regarded monastic seclusion
as a good thing for all. As understood by him,

the monastery was something quite different to what it has become in a later age. He aimed by his teaching and example to revive, as far as possible, the spirit that inspired it when, as he reminds us with truth, "from our midst went forth the real workers for the people"; when the rule of monastic life was, "he that laboureth not, neither shall he eat"; when the humblest monk was not afraid to rebuke the sin of the powerful; and when the people rightly looked on the monastery as their succourer in trouble, their home in poverty, their encourager in good, and their shield from spiritual and worldly danger. He did not consider the real work of the monastery to be restricted to its four walls. The faithful monk must labour in the world as well as pray in his cell. In this spirit he commands Alexis, after his death, to leave the monastery: "Thou shalt go forth from these walls, and thou shalt live in the world as a monk."

The more we study the actual condition of the Russian people, and the better acquainted we make ourselves with their real wants and desires, the more convinced we must be of the soundness of the views which Dostoevsky all his life advocated with such force and persistency. However strange his defence of monastic institutions, that

have elsewhere outlived their day, may appear to
us, we cannot forget that it is made by one who
knew his country well, was thoroughly versed in
its past and present history, and had closely
identified himself with its best and highest aspirations. There is a homely proverb that tells us,
" What is one people's poison is another people's
food," and I think many of his critics would have
done well if they had borne it in mind, instead of
indulging in wholesale condemnation of the great
novelist as a mystic and a dreamer. We may
admit the mystical tendency of much that he has
written, without taking away aught from his authority. The culture of the so-called intelligent class
in Russia is too void of stability, too ready in its
acceptance of any theory that is at all attractive,
either from its novelty or its plausibility, to afford
a solid basis of national weal and happiness. All
that is sure and firm in the structure of Russian
civilisation is to be found in the life of the people,
the unartificial product of ages, and whose roots
have sunk deep into a soil naturally favourable to
its growth. In spite of the changes that life has
undergone, and the inconsiderate attempts that
have from time to time been made to give it a
new shape, all that is good and sound in it always
has been and still is intimately bound up with the

monastery. It is the monastery, and the monastery alone, that till now wages the people's war against violence. In the days of serfdom it was the peasant's one place of flight and refuge ; in the later days of his comparative freedom it is his one safeguard against lawless encroachment on his rights.

It may be that Dostoevsky has somewhat idealised monastic life, though he is by no means blind to the shortcomings with which it is too often disfigured, and has placed, side by side with Zozime and Alexis, the monk Therapont, who, himself the slave of low superstition, would bind others with the like heavy chains of ignorance and fear. But there is a buoyancy of faith in his grasp and conception of life which gives us courage to try and find order in disorder, robs evil and misery of their power to crush men with despair, enables us to confront with boldness the " doubtful doom of humankind," and endows us with sight to discern the spirituality of a universe that would otherwise be voiceless and meaningless. His is the gospel of hope, the creed of progress, that not only lends us encouragement to advance, but points out the way we should go, and puts into our hand the staff of religious faith by which we may support and guide our steps.

It is based on the two great principles of obedience
and love, as represented by loyalty to the Tsar
and fidelity to the Church,—the two principles
which, I believe, every unprejudiced observer of
Russia will agree with me must underlie any
scheme of reform that is to prove lasting and
profitable. It may be summed up in the stirring
words of Nekrasoff, of all modern poets the one
most in accord with the spirit that leavens the life
of the Russian people :—

" We can no more live as we have lived, cheated by false
    learning,
With dull weariness at soul and chilling cold at heart,
Without the glow of youth, the faith that alone gives life,
Without the sharp pains and the still sharper joys of love,
Without the tears of pity, and the cheerful laugh of
    sympathy,
In the joyless pleasures and idleness of easy wealth.
No, friends, no ! We can no more live as we have lived.
The dark night of unbelief can never bring us rest or ease ;
Men are sick of false promises and jangling calumny;
Our dulled eyes yearn for the sun's illuming ray,
And our tired spirits hunger for the Divine ! "

LECTURE V.

COUNT LEO NICHOLAEVITCH TOLSTOI.

IT is now more than ten years since Count Tolstoi, having already made good his claim to rank highest among the first novelists of Europe, formally announced his abandonment of the work of artist, and the necessity which he felt of henceforth devoting himself to the study of the real meaning and true purpose of life. We all know to what harsh criticisms and ridicule he has been exposed for thus renouncing his calling as artist and busying himself with questions that lie beyond the province of practical life, and whose solution, supposing them to be soluble, can bring no immediate profit.

But Count Tolstoi's critics apparently forget that the novelist, who would be something more than a writer of sensational stories, is, from the nature of his art, bound to analyse the motives, to sound the souls of the characters he creates, and to discover the harmonising principle that underlies their most contradictory and impulsive acts.

It was impossible, therefore, that, in the course of his work, he should not be fronted with those questions that from time to time flit across the mind and arrest the attention of the most vacant and careless amongst us. He could not help asking himself, what is the law and aim of that life, whose varying phases he has sketched in the conduct and career of the different heroes of his romances. Nor was he able to find escape from these thoughts, as most of us do, in the daily occupations of ordinary life, which have little or nothing in common with the spiritual problem of human existence ; but, as I have already suggested, each return to his special work served only to fix his mind more intently on a subject that forms the very essence of his art. Any explanation we can offer will, of course, prove unsatisfactory to those who think the artist has no business to meddle with philosophy, but the fact remains the same. " I found it impossible," he tells us, " to continue living as I had been without a thought of the future ; for I felt too sharply and too clearly that each of the many comforts I enjoyed was purchased at the price of suffering and deprivation to millions of my fellow-creatures." And if this discontent and these doubts as to whether the cravings of his higher nature could find their full satisfaction in the kind of life he was accustomed to lead did not bring him to open and declared revolt against the social creed of the world till a comparatively late period in his career, they had for a long time, and it may be unconsciously, been working in his soul, and their origin is to be found in the surrounding circumstances of his youth and early manhood. Naturally disposed to serious thought, there could be no bond of sympathy between him and the light-minded worldly circle in which he was brought up. Any idea of moral obligation rising from our mutual relations one to another, or any conception of the duties the rich are under towards the poor, were foreign to the code of those with whom he was called on to mix, and a formal observance of the rites of the Church, coupled with a punctilious obedience to the rules of worldly propriety, had, with them, usurped the place of religion. "With all my soul," he writes, " I wished to be good, but I was young, had all the passions of youth, and I was alone, utterly alone, in my search after the good. Each time I ventured to speak of what constituted my heart's one desire,—the wish to become morally good,—I encountered contemptuous looks and mocking rejoinders."

When once this question, What is the meaning

of life, whence does it come, whither does it tend?
has taken hold of the mind, it cannot be stifled or
put aside, but must be answered or bring us to
despair. So long as the puzzle of life, with all its
potential happiness and little achievement, its
fitful aspirations and frequent debasement, its
mysterious suggestions and halting response, presented itself to his mind with no greater force
or persistency than it does to the man who is content to live without thinking why he lives, Count
Tolstoi, as he himself confesses, could find pleasure
and even satisfaction in his poetical creations, and
could look on the world through the mirror of art.
But in proportion as each day he became more
and more convinced that his life was purposeless,
art in itself gradually lost its power to afford him
either enjoyment or profit. It was impossible for
him to go on giving to the world, as though it
were the whole message he had to deliver, what he
had already proved and found to be imperfect and
incomplete.

We have, then, no reason to reproach Count
Tolstoi, because, when the truth was forced upon
him that the life, which he, in common with
thousands of others, was leading, involves the
betrayal and degradation of our higher nature, he
set himself to the task of discovering a higher rule

that should reveal the end and purpose of our life, ·
supply the motive force that can alone give harmonious persistency to our acts, and, by discovering to us what is man's real work in the world,
convert despair into hope, and unbelief into faith.
But we are told that the philosophy he preaches is
merely the crude theorising of an inexperienced
thinker, who imagines that he has discovered
America, but who has simply reproduced ideas of
mediæval devotees, which, if carried into practice,
would destroy all social order, and, from their
fantastic Utopian character, are unworthy of serious
criticism. Of course, Count Tolstoi, whether
writing a novel or propounding a scheme of moral
philosophy, remains true to his artistic nature and ·
instincts. He will give a concrete rather than an
abstract shape to his speculations, and will appeal
to the heart rather than to the mind; nor have we
any right to demand from him the formal and
passionless reasoning of a specialist. But, because
here and there we may detect a flaw in the treatment and exposition of his moral creed, the real
worth of his work is not thereby touched, or the
authority it possesses as a whole impaired. He is
no professed teacher, whose chief anxiety is that
the faultless symmetry of the scheme in favour
with the particular school he belongs to should be

preserved; but he speaks as one who knows he has a gospel to preach, and the unselfish earnestness that inspires his every word compels the most careless and indifferent to listen to his message. We may dispute this or that point in his teaching, but we cannot withhold our admiration and our love from one who has dared to brave the scorn of the world by acting up to the creed he asks us to accept, and renouncing those superfluities with which his rank and position had rendered him familiar, has made himself one with his peasants, and, like them, earns his bread by the sweat of his brow and the labour of his hands.

Like a true artist, he deduced his principles, not from any preconceived self-evolved theory, but from the facts of life. In them, if anywhere, must be found the answer to his doubts and questionings. From his own circle it need scarcely be said he could learn nothing, since, as he has told us, "in our world a man may live for years and have no idea that he is living among Christians, though all the while he may without reproach profess himself to be a Christian and a member of the orthodox Church." He then tried to find the truth he was seeking in intercourse with the literary leaders and representatives of his country, but could not accept their proposed solutions of his difficulties, because their practical inefficiency was forced upon him by the fact that the lives of those who advanced them were in contradiction to their teaching. "These people were repugnant to me," he complains, "and I perceived that their teaching was a lie." The thoroughness of the man, to which we may attribute the extraordinary influence he exercises over the mind and life of young Russia, is strikingly exhibited in this rejection of doctrines that are not, or cannot be, applied to the daily conduct of men. He does not believe that any moral or religious creed, unless it be fully and literally carried out by those who profess it, can possibly effect any good on their own lives or on the world at large.

Disappointed in his attempt to find in these two spheres of life any solid foundation for hope or belief, he came to doubt the possibility of tracing in the mixed condition of things the hand of a Supreme Ruler, to see nothing but inexplicable chaos and confusion in the process of the world, to look upon man as the toy and plaything of an unknowable and irresponsible Power, and more than once he was tempted to solve the riddle of existence by some sudden act of violence. "A man can only consent to live," he writes in reference to these days of scepticism and despair, "so long as he is drunk with the desire of life, but when he comes to himself is forced to confess that it is all a cheat. The horror of my position consisted in the knowledge that all I had done in the past, all that I might do in the present, must be foolishness, useless to myself, and profitless to others." None of us can hope to escape these accesses of despair, but it is only a weak nature that can find satisfaction in negation, or acquiesce in the futility of seeking a rational explanation of life. Accordingly, Count Tolstoi studied the theories of the principal thinkers of Europe, and sought an answer to his doubts in science or in speculative philosophy. The doctrines of individual development and of human progress appeared to him to give no final or adequate solution. So long as growth continues, the hope of unravelling the mystery of life may seem to be attainable, and our work in the world may have a meaning. But ere long the individual returns to the dust whence he originally sprang, leaving nothing behind him, and in the same way human states, societies, and generations are fated to decay and death. The crude dogmas of materialism and the vague assurances of happiness to be found in human progress equally failed to remove the difficulties he had to meet. The one condemn us to the abandonment of all hope, since with our corporeal dissolution will also come the end to all our doubts and questions.   The other hold out a vague promise of their being cleared up somewhere and at some future period, whereas life in the actual present is a cruel mockery, unless the answer be given here and now, and the meaning of life be made known to us, whilst we still have the will to comprehend its demands and the power to accomplish its work.

Science not only furnished no answer, but frankly avowed that none can be given, and that man must rest contented in his ignorance.   This, however, Count Tolstoi could not do, and pursuing his inquiries, found partly in the critical philosophy of Kant and partly in the psychological speculations of English thinkers, the groundwork of a rational and consistent theory of life.   We have already seen how he felt that the theory of individual development can explain life only so long as growth continues.   This caused him to doubt the independence of reason from organic processes, and consequently its competency to decide questions concerning the end and meaning of life.   Reason, the product of life, cannot embrace or explain life, its producer, and of which it is an element and instrument.   It can only explain the manifestations of life so far as they are limited by time and space. So long as we confine ourselves to this restricted sphere, we may appeal to reason, and the single answer it can give is that life has no meaning. But the conception of the finite and the limited necessitates the conception of the infinite and the unlimited. And without this conception, not only is morality impossible, as Kant teaches us, but without it there can be no conscious rational life. It is the foundation of life, life itself. Now, if the infinite is undemonstrable by reason, and if at the same time the idea of the infinite can alone give a meaning to life, it follows that we must seek the answer in that which is wider in its sphere of action, namely, in life.

It will, of course, be understood that the solution to the problem, though to be sought in life, is not to be learned in the life of every man or of every class. We must look for it among those whose actual practical life is based, it may be consciously or it may be without knowledge, on the necessary recognition of, and belief in, the infinite. Nor need we be surprised or discouraged if we find in these lives much ignorance and superstition. It is the province of reason to sweep away the rubbish that encrusts the pure

seed we are in search of, the knowledge of the
end and meaning of life, the knowledge that
transforms life from a burden and evil into the
greatest blessing-and joy to man, the knowledge
that destroys within us the fear of death, and
gives us strength to support suffering, deprivation,
and disappointment.

In a famous passage, that has been quoted so
often that I need not cite it at length, Count
Tolstoi has related by what gradual steps, when
once convinced that the true solution to his
perplexities lay in life itself, he came to discover
which class of men, the cultured, the learned, or
the poor, lead the life that can alone satisfy the
complex requirements of our nature.   He soon
perceived, though at first somewhat confusedly,
that the truth had been hidden from him, not
because he had reasoned falsely, but because his
life had been passed under conditions of luxury,
indolence, and pleasure, that rendered it impossible for it to have any real worth or signification.
It was the same, in some cases still more flagrantly
so, with the lives led by those of his own class and
social position.   And then it was that he began to
examine the life of the people, and, though he
found it to be tainted with more of what he
bluntly calls rubbish than the life of those above

them, there was this great difference between the two : with the latter faith is an accidental quality, an accessory that confers on their life an outward propriety; whilst with the people it constitutes the essence of their lives. Their life is the interpretation of their faith. "In opposition to us, who the wiser we become the less we understand the meaning of life, and think to see some evil mockery in the fate that condemns us to live, to suffer, and to die, these people live, suffer even to death, and die in peaceful resignation, not seldom with an eager joy." As we read these lines, we think of how, in "War and Peace," Pierre, during his captivity, is brought into close relationship with the peasant Karataeff, and learns from him fully and finally the lesson of life ; how, in "Anna Karenina," it is Theodore the peasant who brings Levine to comprehend the way in which men should live, and the real work they have to accomplish in the world; and how, in "The Death of Ivan Ilyitch," the peasant Gerasime inspires the dying man with faith to find light and bliss even in that death he had once awaited with such dread and horror.

The motive and nature of this appeal to the people, as the final authority, has been much misunderstood. I presume there is no occasion

to notice the adverse carpings of his Russian
critics, whose opinions are for the most part
influenced by strong party bias.   But the criticisms of a writer like M. Vogué are, I need
scarcely say, of a quite different order.   In his
most interesting studies on "Les écrivains russes
contemporains," he represents Count Tolstoi as
"being earlier than any other of his fellow-
countrymen, and in a móre marked degree than
any of them, at once the type and interpreter of
that phase of Russian thought which has received
the ugly name of Nihilism."   Now, it may be
safely stated that, in the ordinary and proper
acceptation of the term, Count Tolstoi never was,
and never could be, a Nihilist.   A real Nihilist is
a revolutionary Socialist, a man who denies, but
who has no misgivings as to the necessity of
denying, knows exactly what he is to do, and
finds satisfaction and peace in his denial.   He is,
as Dostoevsky neatly expressed it, "a straight-
lined thinker," and never, even for a moment,
swerves from his track of hard unsympathising
unbelief.   With Count Tolstoi it was the exact
contrary.   He could not make denial the ultimate
stage of thought; he was from first to last haunted
with a keen consciousness of the necessity of
believing; his soul hungered for the truth, and,

though for a while the search seemed to him to be vain and fruitless, he never completely lost the hope of attaining it; and the final call to faith in God was the only possible outcome of these earlier stages of doubt and despair. It is an equally grave mistake on the part of M. Vogué, when he somewhat petulantly rejects the religious creed of Count Tolstoi because there is nothing original in it, declares it to be a *mélange* of fables of the middle ages that have from time to time been resuscitated among the Waldenses, the Lollards, and the Anabaptists, and affirms that the only fruit his teaching can bear is the complete renunciation of our intellectual nature, a dull resigned quietism, a fanatically ascetic indifference to the dignity and pleasures of life. We may readily admit its lack of originality, and many will be inclined to regard this as rather a recommendatory quality than a fault. We must not forget that Count Tolstoi has emphatically told us that what he believes in and what he would teach us is "Christ's Christianity," that is, Christianity, not as it has been cunningly toned down in order to bring it into accord with the lives and interests of worldly professors, but in all its bald and naked simplicity as Christ him-self originally taught it. Count Tolstoi, to the annoyance of many of his readers and critics, has an irritating and uncomfortable way of supposing that Christ understood what He meant to say, and he accordingly interprets His precepts in their plain literal sense. To him, as to Alexis Karamazoff, the idea that he could go on living his former life seemed strange and impossible. It had been commanded him to "give all that thou hast, and follow me;" and Alexis said to himself, it will not be enough if, instead of giving "all," I merely give two roubles, or if, instead of "following me," I content myself with attending a certain number of church services. Nor do I suppose that, even if the peculiar doctrines, of which Count Tolstoi has made himself the most consistent exponent in our days, can be traced no farther back than to the Middle Ages, they must therefore necessarily be idle and baseless fables. We cannot be justified in condemning and rejecting them simply because they found acceptance and credence in the so-called Dark Ages. The only question we need busy or concern ourselves with is, Are they true, and do they form an essential constituent of the faith we profess to hold as the guide and rule of life? And whatever error there may be in them, they are at least free from the taint of asceticism. As we have already seen, in Count Tolstoi's creed, belief in the infinite is a necessity of life, without which life is an impossibility and unthinkable. Our individual earthly life is, therefore, perfect only so far as it is brought into harmony with the law of the infinite, and to fulfil that law constitutes our highest bliss and greatest happiness. We cannot, then, despise or neglect this life; asçeticism is no longer a virtue, but a revolt against nature, and the true pleasures of life, instead of being shunned as hurtful and seductive, are to be cultivated and enjoyed. But what most displeases M. Vogué, is that Pierre Bezouchoff, the well-bred, accomplished aristocrat, should find a teacher in the rude Karataeff, and learn from a simple peasant the lesson of life. "This Karataeff," he writes, "endures all the sufferings of his harsh captivity with the quiet and humble resignation of a beast of burden; addresses to him a few simple words, chiefly composed of popular proverbs that have little defined meaning and are inspired by a tone of abnegation, brotherhood, and a peculiar fanaticism; one evening, when he has grown so weak that he can march no farther, he is shot down by a soldier of the convoy and left to die beneath a snow-covered fir-tree, and he accepts his fate in the same equable, uncomplaining spirit as he would have met any other accident of life, like some sick dog, or, to speak more justly, like some dumb brute." What, however, strikes the cultured critic as so strange and unreal, will appear to Count Tolstoi, and those best acquainted with the high qualities of the peasant class in Russia, to be very simple and quite natural. No doubt, when sketching to us the character of Karataeff, the novelist was thinking of the un-lettered Soutaieff, one of those unguided but honest gropers after truth who, dissatisfied with the cold dogmatism of the official Church, and tired of being held in leading-strings, dare to read and think for themselves, and from whom, we know, Count Tolstoi more than once sought counsel and advice. The power which Soutaieff obtained over those to whom he spoke, with that simplicity which so offends the critic because it is couched in the proverb language of the people, is proved by the rapidity with which his creed has spread throughout the villages of southern Russia. Among his earliest converts was a younger brother, who, sharing his opinions on the iniquity of war, refused to serve in the army. For this offence he was, of course, arrested and marched off, in company with a number of recruits less scrupu-lous than himself, to be tried before a court-martial. But, before they reached their destination, he had already converted many to his creed. To prevent his doing further mischief he was quickly judged and sentenced to hard labour for life in the mines of Siberia. And in his exile, without a murmur at the harshness of his lot, he continued his good work, and more than one convict has had reason to bless the day when he was first brought into contact with the peasant evangelist of Tver. Karataeff is one of these. To some of us he may be a puzzle and enigma, but we do wrong to affect contempt for men who, through long ages of oppression and neglect, have pre-served a simpleness of mind that enables them to endure all in the full assurance that it is God's will, and that in due time he will bring all to a foreordained end,—the overthrow of evil and the triumph of good. "Do not fret," he says to Pierre on the first day of his imprisonment, "we suffer for an hour, but we live for ever." In these words we have summed up the whole faith of the Russian peasant.

It is by this process, this appeal to the people, that Count Tolstoi arrives at the formulation of a series of moral laws that lie at the basis of all his teaching and flow necessarily from his theory of life. They are six in number, and are as follows :—Do not war. Do not judge. Do not

commit fornication.   Do not swear.   Do not give
way to anger.   Do not óppose with force the
evildoer.

With the exception of the first and sixth precepts, this moral code does not call for any special
remark.   And, in reference to the first, I must
not dwell at any length on Count Tolstoi's sharp
denunciation of all war as a folly and a crime, lest
I should give a political colouring to lectures
which are designed to be of an exclusively literary
character.   I would only observe that his righteous
protests against the hideous cruelties and wrongs
committed in the name of patriotism and honour
serve to bring out the fearless honesty of the man,
living, as he does, in a country where the military
element is dominant and rules with such crushing
power.   His views are in thorough accordance
with those which the great orator, whose loss
England has so lately had occasion to deplore,
was wont to advocate, and rather than abandon
which he willingly sacrificed place and popularity.
And as with John Bright, so with Count Tolstoi ;
what chiefly moves his anger and indignation is
that the Church and her priests should bless and
sanction what it is their duty to curse and
denounce.   "Make war," he exclaims, "but not
in the name of Christ, the Herald of Peace, but in

the name of the devil, who alone is the god of war." Men of the world, I know, regard the belief that wars will cease and be replaced by some humaner and more rational mode of settling international quarrels as a harmless but idle fancy; but it seems to me that we are justified in holding fast to the hope that the law of violence and brute force will ere long yield to a gentle and juster law. No salutary reform has ever been effected in the lives of men or nations, which, when first proposed, was not hotly ridiculed by wise and practical men as foolish and impossible of realisation. He who, some seventy years ago, had declared that, in this country at least, duelling would soon cease to be considered a sensible way of avenging an insult, would certainly have been stigmatised as a madman and a dreamer.

But of the six rules of life laid down for us by Count Tolstoi, it is the sixth, forbidding us to oppose by force the evildoer, that has most provoked angry criticism and contemptuous laughter. Nor is it difficult, if we so choose, to turn it into ridicule. And to prove its absurdity, some of his critics, who failed to see how intimately bound up the law is with the fundamental principles of morality, have been pleased to imagine extreme cases, as, for example, the defence against lawless violence of one's own life, or the life of one near and dear to us.   Count Tolstoi, by way of reply, in one of his shorter stories has condemned the hero for shooting a burglar and thereby saving his mother's life.   It may, I think, with reason be doubted whether it is wise to introduce ticklish moral problems of this kind into a tale designed for popular reading, but, if we are to discuss the question, the only conclusion at which we can arrive is that Count Tolstoi is morally right.   A moral law admits of no exception.   Each of the Ten Commandments is an absolute, unconditional prohibition.   The instant the moralist admits that his law may sometimes be disregarded, the law ceases to exist.   We are then driven to search for a principle higher than that on which the law is based, and by whose guidance we may be able to decide in what cases and under what circumstances disobedience to it is permitted.   We must not forget, moreover, that an act may be necessary, and so far justifiable, without being consequently moral.   But it is exclusively the moral aspect of the question which Count Tolstoi has in view when he affirms the slayer of the burglar to have committed a crime, or when he declares that to oppose the evil-doer by means of violence is a sin.

It is not by trying to apply it to exceptional cases that we shall discover the significance and worth of this prohibitory law. We may acknowledge that neither in their private nor in their public relations to one another do men make it their universal rule and guide. In this respect it does but share the fate of all moral laws. At the same time, experience teaches us that with each generation its adoption as a principle that should regulate our conduct becomes more general. Of this we have proofs in the changes that have been gradually effected in our system of education, in our treatment of criminals, and in our bearing towards those whose faith differs from our own. We no longer convert with the sword, but by argument; we do not any more punish merely to revenge the wrong done to society; we induce our children to take an intelligent interest in their studies instead of making them look on the schoolroom as a place of torture. Reason reigns where once force and violence tyrannised, and in our age more than ever, to quote the words of Auguste Comte, " Les idées gouvernent et bouleversent le monde."

The views of Count Tolstoi on science and art, which have aroused the hostility of professed specialists to the same extent as his religious

opinions have shocked those who plume themselves on their orthodoxy, are by no means so
sweeping and revolutionary as they are frequently
represented to be. They are the logical consequence of his theological and social creed. Even
if we had never read a line of his elaborate essay
on national education, we should instinctively be
inclined to suspect that the accusation so freely
brought against him by some of his critics, that he
is opposed to the study and spread of science,
must be founded on a gross misconception. There
is a manifest contradiction of ideas, amounting to
absurdity, in the notion that Count Tolstoi, himself one of the most highly cultured and widely
read men of his country, should at the same time
be the apologist for ignorance, the sworn foe of
knowledge. It is not against science that he
directs his attack, but against the false application
of science. "The sphere of general human
knowledge," he writes, " is all but boundless, and,
before a man sets to study a thing, he must assure
himself that the subject he has chosen is important for him, and of more importance than all
the subjects of knowledge with which he is
surrounded, and he must determine why he has
selected this in preference to the others." In
these words he protests against acquiring know-

ledge for mere knowledge sake, and exalts the use of knowledge above knowledge in itself. "The thinker and the artist," he continues, "should not sit quietly on some Olympian height, but they must suffer together with their fellow creatures, if they would find for themselves or others escape from or consolation in suffering. Science and art will only then be of use to the people when, living among the people and like the people, the thinker and artist, claiming neither rights nor privileges, shall make them sharers in their learning and art."

Nor are these words mere commonplace as they may, perhaps, seem to be to the English reader. To understand them fully we must bear in mind the actual condition and wants of the Russian people. Even in the cities and larger towns, till within a very recent period, and only since Count Tolstoi and the few who belong to what is called the Tolstoi school began to write, little or nothing has been done to make the masses acquainted with the wonders of modern science, or to apply its discoveries to the bettering and improvement of their lot. The homes of the poor are unhealthy and ill-drained; amusements of a rational kind do not exist for them; workmen's clubs are still a thing unknown; the theatres are virtually closed to all save the middle and upper classes ; and the public-house is the only place of recreation and enjoyment open to the *moujik*.

And if it be true, as we so often hear, that the people are unfitted through their ignorance and hereditary tastes to take pleasure in anything but vulgar and noisy shows, and that Ivan's highest idea of enjoyment is to get dead drunk, this only proves the incompleteness and inefficiency of the system of national education actually in force.   As Count Tolstoi has pointed out in the essay I have already alluded to, all are agreed that the people ought to be taught; but the real question we have to decide is, what we should teach them. This involves the further question, who is to determine what the people shall be taught ?   In practice we know how this second question is answered. Bureaucratic administrators are too fond of regarding the people as a kind of *tabula rasa*, and accordingly draw up an elaborate programme of studies, which they proceed to apply indiscriminately to all schools for the children of peasants, in the belief that their scheme will not only bear good fruit, but will be gratefully and eagerly adopted.   But, in reality, the people have already their religion, their language, and even their favourite literature, and any scheme that is to prove useful or acceptable must be founded on their culture and be in harmony with their religious ideas. We have not to create; we have only to encourage and aid the growth and development of what already exists. It is in consequence of the neglect of these elementary principles that so little success has hitherto attended the well-meant, but ill-organised, attempts that have been made to raise the existing low level of popular education in Russia. The people have no need to be told what they want, and if we wish the education of the people to become a reality and not simply a formal paper-scheme,—if we wish to overcome their stubborn indifference to learning and instruction, which is the result of a suspicious fear that, by forcing on them a system of our own, we are pursuing some selfish end rather than seeking their good,—we must let them conduct their schools after their own ideas, with as little interference as possible on our part, and in accordance with the traditions and necessities of the peasant class.

Owing to the peculiar conditions of Russian life, the instruction given to women and the social position they occupy have in that country more than elsewhere a close connexion with, and an immediate bearing on, the education and well-being of the peasantry.   It is, therefore, the more strange that Count Tolstoi persistently ignores the fact that the welfare of the peasantry is bound up with the recognition of the natural rights of women, and has ranked himself among the advocates of the complete subordination of the woman to man.   Saint Paul himself is not more emphatic in restricting her to the narrowest sphere of action, and he would seem to think that the province of a woman's duty is confined to waiting on her husband, bearing children, and minding the kitchen.   In support of an opinion which, I need scarcely say, is contradictory to past experience and discordant with the future, Count Tolstoi appeals to the Bible, and quotes the curse pronounced on the human race after the fall, by which man is condemned to eat his bread in the sweat of his brow, and woman to bring forth children in sorrow.   But Count Tolstoi forgets that, though it be impossible for us to free ourselves entirely from the primal curse,—that is, in other words, the law of nature,—it is within our power to mitigate its force, and that by failing to do so we declare ourselves to be passive fatalists and idly forego the exercise of the will with which nature has endowed us.   By the adoption of his theory, which is fundamentally at variance with his religious creed, we bring the women of Russia back to the old days, when, to cite the words of Belinsky, "men, in conditions and classes of Russian society, occupied the first rank, but we cannot say that women occupied the second or even an inferior rank, since, to tell the truth, they in reality occupied no rank at all." Of the humiliations and degradation to which, in those evil days, women were subjected, Ostrovsky has given a terrible but unexaggerated picture in his different dramas. Besides, whoever else may claim with consistency to plead for the denial to his countrywomen of the simplest and most elementary right, the right to be educated, Count Tolstoi has completely put himself out of court. If, in the case of the peasantry, he argues that the education of their children, since they themselves are directly interested in it, should be left to their own discretion and management, instead of being arbitrarily directed by a body of official *tchinov-niks*, the same argument applies with equal force to women. We may be quite sure, if Russian women demand higher instruction than has hither-to been given them, and crowd the few institutions where it can be had, it is because they feel the urgent necessity of it, and are the best judges of what they want. Nor is there any reasonable fear of their being unsexed by having free play granted to their natural faculties.

The position taken up by Count Tolstoi on this question is the more to be regretted when we recollect the extraordinary difficulties with which the promoters of Medical Courses and Higher Classes for the instruction of women have had to contend. The sneers he indulges in at the expense of women, who, as he alleges, shirk the duties of wives and mothers that they may occupy themselves with nerve phenomena and differentials, must not blind us to the good which these institutions have already during the short time of their existence effected. The number of scholars attending the Higher Classes at St. Petersburg in 1885, the year from which the admission of new pupils has been forbidden, amounted to about 1,100, and of these 85 per cent. finished the full course, extending over four years, and passed the final examination. The Medical Courses in St. Petersburg alone turn out yearly from forty to fifty competent and well-qualified practitioners. In proof of the sympathy with which these courses are regarded by the Russian public, I may mention that when, six years ago, it was proposed to close them on the plea that the Government had not sufficient means to support them, subscriptions amounting to more than five times the sum required were without any difficulty raised,—a merchant at Moscow giving not less than 100,000 roubles, and seven lady donors of the same city contributing 50,000 roubles each.

It is in the remoter provinces of Russia that the majority of these women, on quitting the classes, have proved what influence their studies have had on their character and conception of life. It should also be remembered at what a cost in a large number of cases these studies were pursued. Many came from enormous distances to Moscow or St. Petersburg, the only cities where the classes exist, some even making the long journey on foot; and in order to find the necessary fees devoted the few free evening hours they had to work as teachers, copyists, or translators. Nor was there any brilliant future awaiting them, to tempt them to make such sacrifices or to endure these privations. Prompted by the single unselfish desire to come to the help of the ignorant and necessitous, they voluntarily accompanied the troops in the late war with Turkey and served as sisters of mercy on the field and in the hospitals; accepted ill-paid places as doctors in what the Russians aptly call the "deaf and dumb" districts of the empire, where the want of experienced practitioners is most severely felt, and where the sick, for lack of attendance, are left to die like flies ; or occupied themselves as school teachers in villages, where, but for them, the peasantry must have remained uninstructed and uncared for. And if the tone of home life, as most undoubtedly is the case, in those classes of society whence Ostrovsky liked to take his characters, has lost not a little of the savageness and indelicacy that characterised it up to a period within the memory of us all, the change in the relation between man and wife, parents and children, is largely due to the healthy influence exercised on their circle by women who have received a broader culture and wider knowledge than could be obtained in the old days, when the rude patriarchal system of family life prevailed.

We have now gone through the main points of Count Tolstoi's religious and social creed. Many may not be disposed to accept it in its every detail, or exactly in the shape in which it has been presented to us ; but there are few, I think, who will care to dispute its stimulating influence or its coherency with the best ideas and spirit of our age. He would stir us from the cowardly fear of being true to ourselves, and wean us from the passive adoption of certain rules of life, by which we are content to regulate our conduct without once inquiring whether they are good or bad, simply because they are acknowledged by the generality of men, and their non-observance might expose us to the suspicion of being unpractical and eccentric. To this spiritual lethargy he traces the emptiness of the life we lead, the insincerity of our beliefs, the want of a common active tie that shall bind man to man and make the interests of each the interests of all. He believes, and would have us believe, in man's capacity to realise the ideal of human nature. That ideal is with Count Tolstoi no idle phrase, but lies within our grasp, and he himself, before holding it up as the end to which we should aim, has proved and tested its worth. The obligation under which each of us lies to take an active share in the common battle of life and in the common struggle with nature; simplicity and truthfulness in our speech and acts; an intelligent consistency and moderation in the satisfaction of our wants and desires; a free, unrestrained, brotherly bond of sympathy and interest between individuals and between the different classes of society,—this sums up the formula of his ideal.

I have said that Count Tolstoi's teaching is in accord with the tendencies and ideas of the age in which we live. It is the product of the nineteenth century. Its fundamental principle is the equality of all in presence of the one universal law: labour and eat. This principle is the outcome and higher application of the democratic spirit that underlies every branch and phase of our modern life. But whilst the democratic idea of our days is social and utilitarian, that of Count Tolstoi's creed is individual and ethical. Instead of regarding work as a necessary condition of social happiness and general progress, he teaches us that only by work and by physical labour can man attain the full development of his nature, and secure his own personal happiness. The union between the happiness of mankind as a whole and the happiness of man as an individual is thus established, and the attainment of the one guarantees the attainment of the other.

In attempting to lay before you a brief summary of Count Tolstoi's moral and social philosophy, I have been obliged to repeat much of what I said in a course of lectures I had the privilege of delivering last year at the Royal Institution. Now, as then, I can only conclude by expressing a hope that, however imperfectly I may have acquitted myself of the task, I have not altogether failed to inspire you with something of that grateful love I feel for a writer from whom I have learned so much, and to whom I must ever remain indebted for having dispelled more than one disquieting doubt, and made the end and meaning of our human lives clear, rational, intelligible. In one of his essays, the late Matthew Arnold assured us that before long the English would all be studying Russian that they might read Tolstoi. Should any of those whom I am addressing be tempted to do so from what they have heard to-day, I am convinced they will have no reason to regret the labour or trouble they may have to encounter in mastering the difficulties of the Russian language.

LECTURE VI.

VSEVOLOD GARSCHINE AND VLADIMIR KOROLENKO.

THE writers of whom I have had occasion to speak in the preceding lectures, have all acquired a European celebrity, but the names of M. Garschine and M. Korolenko are, I imagine, scarcely known beyond the limits of their own country. In one of his letters, Tourgenieff speaks of Garschine in the following terms: "Of all our young writers, he is the one that gives most promise of a brilliant future. He has all the qualities of real genius; an artistic temperament, a keen and clear observation of human nature and individual character, an accurate sense of proportion, simplicity, and beauty of style, and, as a result of all this, a rare and striking originality." In judging how far the promises of Tourgenieff discerned in the young writer, just then beginning his literary career, were fulfilled, we must, of course, bear in mind the haunting fear of a recurrence of the most terrible of all maladies that embittered his whole life, and the early age at which he died. Admira-

tion at what he achieved, rather than disappointment that he did not accomplish more, will then
be the feeling with which we close our study of
the two small volumes containing all that he ever
wrote.

Vsevolod Michaelovitch Garschine was born, '
February 2, 1855, on the estate of his grandmother,
in the government of Ekaterinoslaff. The details
that have been made public concerning his earlier
years are few and scanty. His childhood, from
causes into which it is not necessary to enter, was
an extremely unhappy one, and the lasting impressions left on his mind by the rough treatment
he was exposed to will explain certain peculiarities
in his character and views of life. In his ninth
year he was sent up to St. Petersburg, and placed
at one of the public schools. As a youth he was
shy and reserved, exhibited little liking for the
ordinary games and amusements of boyhood, was
passionately fond of reading, and, as one who
knew him well has told us, "lived in a world of
his own." It was whilst at school he exhibited the
first signs of abnormal nervous excitability, which,
before long, developed into pronounced mental
derangement, and rendered it necessary to place
him under the care of Dr. Frei, the director of a
private asylum. Towards the end of 1873, his

health was sufficiently re-established to justify his removal, and, having passed the final gymnasium examination, he entered the Mining Corps. There would seem to have been no particular reason for his choosing this establishment, since he had already resolved to adopt the literary calling, and during his stay there busied himself but little with the specially technical subjects included in the programme of studies. One of his fellow students, M. Maliescheff, relates how Garschine was the originator and founder of the so-called " Friday Evenings," at which literary papers were read and discussed, and questions relating to art and life were debated, at times with all the warmth and passion natural to youthful disputants. It was at one of these meetings that he read his story, " Four Days," which, however, was not published till 1878, and with which, though he had previously written for a St. Petersburg paper a short series of criticisms on art, his career as a novelist really commences.

But those were troublous days. To a man of Garschine's eager sensitiveness it was impossible to remain a passive spectator of the cruelties then being enacted in Bulgaria, and no sooner were the first Russian troops called to arms to avenge the sufferings of their Slav brethren, than he threw up his mining studies and enlisted as a volunteer.

" Many thanks," he writes in a letter to a friend,
"for your scientific news, but, to tell you the
truth, Teploff's electrophore and the coalition of
chemical and physical atoms interest me far less
than the terrible fact that the Turks have massa-
cred thirty thousand defenceless old men, women,
and children. A plague on all your learned
societies, if with all their grand scientific theories
they are unable to render the accomplishment of
such horrors an impossibility. If you only knew
how my heart boils within me ! If I am not ill
again this summer it will be a miracle ! " His
example was followed by more than one of his
fellow-students, and together with them he set
out, May 1, 1877, to join the active army at
Kiescheneff.

What he saw and experienced during that
eventful campaign, in which, it may be remarked,
he behaved with more than creditable bravery,
forms the subject of his first two stories, "Four
Days" and " Memoirs of a Private Soldier." The
daily horrors he witnessed, the sight of wounded
men dying in slow agony, the cries and fear of
flying villagers leaving their homes behind them a
prey to flames, fertile fields transformed into
savage wastes, the foul crimes committed by
a rude soldiery drunk with victory, — all this

N

produced on him an enduring sense of the sin of
war, and led him in his different tales to plead
the cause of peace with a simple earnestness that
speaks the strength and sincerity of his convictions. In a letter to M. Maliescheff he writes :—
"Some of the corpses we saw were truly horrible :
one Turk, instead of being buried, had been en-
veloped in straw and burned by the Cossacks,
and there lay a black charred mass of something
that bore in its outlines a faint resemblance to a
human body. In many places the clefts were
spotted with bits of red flesh. Here, a dissevered
skull in which the white pearly teeth stood out
clearly on a black ground ; there, a heap of bones
let loose from the shattered broken joints." In
an engagement near Ayaslar he was severely
wounded and was sent home. The two or three
years he now spent partly at Kharkoff and partly
at St. Petersburg were, perhaps, the happiest of his
life. He quickly established his claim to rank
high among the contemporary novelists of Russia ;
he made acquaintance, which, in many cases,
ripened into close intimacy, with the leading
artists and writers of his country; and those
brought into communication with him remarked
that he now began to acquire an evenness and
cheerfulness of temperament that seemed to indi-

cate a complete and permanent recovery of health.
But these hopes were destined soon to be frus-
trated. Before long his malady returned, and
once more his friends were obliged to place him
under restraint. The accesses of folly alternated
with short intervals of undisturbed intelligence,
and these snatches of fitful consciousness were
even fuller of torture and agony than the periods
of raving passionate frenzy. For with them came
back the clear and distinct recollection of all the
wild words he had uttered and all the senseless
acts he had committed in his madness. And
when, after two years' confinement, he was allowed
to quit the asylum, he wrote his story, "The Red
Flower," in which he has recorded all that he
thought, felt, and fancied during those long
months of mental derangement. "I still live,—
at least, I suppose, it is the only expression I can
use," he writes in a letter to M. Maliescheff;
"though, to speak more truly, I no longer live.
My bodily organs still act and perform their
ordinary functions; I eat, I sleep, I get up, and
then I eat and sleep again. As to thinking, I
scarcely think at all, and, it must be confessed, it
is better not to think, for any train of thought into
which I am led is torturing and revolting. There
are those who imagine that a man with a diseased

brain does not know what he is doing; but my own experience has taught me it is not so. At any rate, what we call conscience torments me for all I did in madness as sharply as it ever could have tortured me had I never been mad."

I do not envy the man who can read the story of the last seven years of Garschine's life and remain untouched. A deep melancholy, which could be cast off only at rare intervals to return with increased force, fell upon him and poisoned his every pleasure and employment. "A heavy stone," to quote the words of an unfinished tale that has never been published, "lay upon his heart; the heart could not bear its weight, but broke." In 1883 he married, but a true wife's devotion and loving care had no power to rouse him from his despair, or dispel the constant racking pain with which his aching head throbbed and beat. For hours he would sit, silent and motionless, and, in reply to any offer of help, would raise his hand to his head, as if imploring relief of some ill he was unable to define or explain. He gradually lost all hope, all faith. He began to hear mysterious sounds and voices, and would hurriedly run from room to room to escape the pursuing phantoms of a sick brain. And then came the end. Early one March morning, in 1888, he

crept unobserved from his room, rushed to the
landing of the staircase leading down into the hall,
and, throwing himself over the balustrade, was
found lying on the stone floor, with one of his
legs broken and his face terribly disfigured. He
was immediately removed to the neighbouring
hospital in a state of semi-consciousness. As he
was being placed in the carriage that was to con-
vey him there, he pressed his hand to his heart,
and said: "Why trouble about the leg? the
pain is here"; and when his friends carried him
into the room assigned him and laid him gently
on the bed, he looked round with a smile, and
muttered, "Thank God!" as if glad to have
reached the last station in his short, sad life-
journey. With these words, his head sank back
on the pillow, he feebly raised his hand and tried
to make the sign of the Cross on his breast, gave a
faint sigh, and all was over. The "heavy stone,"
of which he so often complained, had been taken
away, and ceased to weigh upon his heart.

In choosing the form of fiction as the vehicle
for expressing his ideas and revealing the working
of his mind, not only in its normal condition, but
still oftener in its uncontrolled aberrations, Garschine has afforded a direct proof of his rare sensi-
tivenesss to the impressions of life. He did not

possess the patience or self-command necessary to set forth any of the manifestations of life circumstantially and in detail. He felt too strongly to attempt this, and was eager to free himself as quickly as possible from the all-absorbing impression produced upon him by the incident or train of thought he happened to be describing. The need of relief from this torturing sensibility to the facts of life was all the stronger, because he never could separate the individual fact from the general order of life, and, in the singular event, he invariably recognised the revelation of the universal law. For this reason, in each of his tales, however short, he collects, compares, and examines the whole sum of phenomena connected with or flowing from the fact of life that first and originally engaged his thoughts.

Of this we have a striking example in the earliest of his stories, " Four Days." Nothing can be more ordinary, more commonplace, than the incident that forms the subject of the whole tale. The hero in a skirmish kills a Turk, and is himself severely wounded, and left to lie four whole days on the field, close to the corpse of the man he had slain. But, by tracing and analysing in their minutest details the trains of thought that succeed each other in the fevered brain of the

wounded man, the novelist, after his wont, makes
the accidental fact serve as a background to the
wider moral question that underlies it.   The fate
of Ivanoff, which, after all, has been the fate of a
hundred Ivanoffs in every military campaign, thus
receives its true significance, which, from its com-
monness, we are likely to overlook, and it reveals,
in all their nakedness, the false pretences and
hypocrisies of our conventional morality.   " Before me lies the man I slew.   And why did I kill
him ?   He lies there, dead, all stained and dirtied
with blood.   Why did a cruel fate drive him
hither ?   Who is he ?   Perchance he, too, like
myself, has an aged mother.   Long will she sit in
the evenings by the door of her rude mud-hut,
peering into the distant North, awaiting the return
of her darling son, her help and bread-winner.
And I ?   It will be the same with me.   Willingly
would I change places with him.   He is happy :
he hears nothing, feels no pain from wounds, no
death-agony, no thirst.   The bayonet-thrust went
home straight to his heart.   Through his uniform I
see a huge black gash, and all around it clotted blood.
And that is *my* work ! "   And then the thoughts
of the abandoned soldier are fixed for a while on
his own sufferings and the hopeless horror of his
position, but soon they get back to their former

current, and once more he is confronted with a
sense of the criminal folly he had been guilty of in
spite of the grand pretentious part he had aped to
play. "All my thoughts are of *him*, and I can
think of nothing else. Is it possible that I abandoned all that was dear and near to me, marched
sore-foot for thousands of miles, endured cold,
hunger, burning heat, and am now lying here in
hideous torment, only that this wretched creature
might cease to live? And, pray, what service
have I rendered to military glory, or to the sacred
cause, beyond this murder? Murder! And who,
then, is the murderer? Why, I myself. When I took
it into my head to serve in the army as a volunteer,
neither my mother nor Masha tried to dissuade me,
though they often wept at my decision. Blinded
with my fantastic idea, I could not see their tears,
I did not understand,—now I understand too well,
—what a wrong I was doing to those who should
have been dearer to me than all the world. But
what good can these thoughts bring me now?
We never can redeem the past. And yet I might
have known this from the strange coldness with
which most of my acquaintances received the
news of my intentions. Poor fellow, he was
always a little queer, you know, else he would
never go and meddle with affairs that do not

concern him ! How could they talk like that, in
flat contradiction to their own ideas of heroism,
love for one's country, and other like high virtues ?
For, of course, in their eyes I could not be other
than the representative of these glorious qualities.
And, nevertheless, I was a little daft, you know.
And so I arrive at Kiescheneff. I don my knap-
sack and all the other military accessories. And
I march with thousands, of whom very few are,
like myself, serving of their own good will. They
would gladly have remained in their homes, if
they had only been allowed. But they trudge on,
just as we, volunteers, trudge on ; they march and
march thousands of miles, and fight, as well as we
do, and even better. They do their duty without
a murmur, though there is scarcely one among
them all who would not throw it all up and return home, — if only they had their own free
way."

There is very little to cheer, nothing to amuse, in
the tales of M. Garschine. They are all coloured
with a melancholy, the reflex of his own sad life.
Thus we cannot help noting that all his stories,
not only his narratives of war, in which there
would be nothing surprising, end sadly. At times
he introduces us into spheres of unmitigated
misery and sin, circles of life that we think right

and proper to ignore, and in speaking of which it certainly requires the greatest delicacy on the part of a writer to prevent his pictures of the real world becoming hurtful and revolting to the moral sense. Take, for example, the second of his tales, "A Catastrophe." The subject is not a pleasing one; it is nothing less than the confessions of a fallen woman. And yet, from beginning to end there is not a false note struck. The story is un-canny, but not unclean. It is one of those few stories that make us think. We read and are made to doubt whether there must not be some-thing wrong in a civilisation that calls itself Chris-tian, and still has no power to extirpate some at least of those glaring vices that grow up and flourish in its very midst. What a picture of despair,—hopeless, brutish submission to her so-called fate,—is presented in the savage, defiant apology Nadejida Nicholaevna makes for keeping to and not caring, even were a chance offered her, to change her life of vice and degradation. "How dull and stupid all this thinking is ! Of course, it is all the same, seeing I cannot change my life. And why cannot I change it? Simply because I do not wish. I have taken to this business, and I know the road I have to go. I remember once seeing a caricature in "Strekoza,"—a comic journal

which a friend of mine often brought me, especially when there was anything in it unusually
droll,—the portrait of a pretty little girl playing
with a doll, and around her two groups of figures
representing the two futures open before her. The
first group was composed of a little school-girl, a
modest young maiden, the mother of a family,
and, lastly, an old woman, but so venerable-
looking ! In the second group, you saw, first, a girl
coming out of a shop with a basket on her arm,
then there was,—myself, and again,—myself, and
once more,—myself. The first I was,—just what
I am now; the second, I, a poor ragged street-
sweeper ; and the third, I, a repulsive, hideous old
hag. But I shall never come to that ! Two or
three years more, if I can only support the life,
and then, to the cemetery. There can be no
other end ; but I am not frightened. . . . And
why should I think of my future, when I already
know too well what it will be ? Why think of my
past, when there is nothing in that past to make
me regret that I cannot exchange my actual life
for it ? That is true. . . . I must stay at my post
and die. But better not to try and think ! I only
know that I am drunk, and that I have no clear
idea of anything. My head is distracted with
strange, confused thoughts, and I mix up in my

mind the dirty saloon where I shall dance to-night and the cell in the lock-up, to get a comfortable night's shelter in which you must be drunk. · My temples throb, my ears tingle, my head is racked with pain, and I feel as if I were being carried down some rushing stream, I know not whither. I try to stop myself, to hold on by anything, by a mere straw ; but, alas ! there is not even a straw by whose help I can keep myself from floating down."

As we might expect from its theme, " The Red Flower " is, of all these tales, the one that leaves the strongest and the weirdest impression on the mind of the reader. It is distinct from and unlike anything else in Russian literature. For it is not, as Gogol's masterpiece, "The Diary of a Madman," a fictitious record of the wild ravings in which the practised student of human nature imagines a madman to indulge, but in it we have the carefully gathered up reminiscences of the strange convulsions of a diseased mind, presented to us, in a form free from all affectations of style, by the very man who had thought the thoughts and felt the feelings he describes.

The novelist sharply distinguishes two periods in his illness. The first is characterised by the absence of any settled order in his delirious fancies, and one wild impulse of mad raving is followed by another without there being any apparent connexion between the trains of ideas. In the second period there is a fixed series of ideas, with which the acts of the madman are closely connected, they being the motors of his activity. On the first day after his admission into the asylum, he had noticed in the little garden, on to which the windows of his room looked, two poppies of a rare kind, and whose bright colour particularly attracted his attention. Each day his confused ideas became more and more concen· trated on these poppies, till at length he conceived the bizarre idea that their flowers contained in themselves the root and essence of all evil, and that, could he but destroy them, he would thereby secure the full and final triumph of good over ill. Henceforth the thoughts of the sick man were exclusively directed to the attainment of this end.

The accuracy with which he notes each phase in his malady is, as we are reminded by Dr. Siekkorsky, who speaks with the authority of one well practised in the treatment of mental diseases, best seen in the description he gives of the coexistence of two consciousnesses, the normal and the pathological. They exist together, but the former is powerless to gain, or even to

struggle for, supremacy. "He knew," writes the
novelist, "that he was in a mad asylum ; he also
knew that he was ill. Sometimes, as on the first
night, he awoke from sleep in the midst of the
quiet that succeeded the day's noise, feeling a
strange ache in all his limbs and a dull heaviness
in his brain, but all the while fully conscious. It
may have been owing to the absence in the silence
of the night and early dawn of all that could excite
or impress him, or it may have been owing to the
feeble action of the brain on his first awakening,
that in such minutes he completely understood
his position, and felt, as it were, in perfect health.
But then day came on, and, together with the
light and stir of life in the asylum, his mind was
again a prey to chance impressions, his sickly
brain could not cope with them, and once more
he lost all control over his reason. The ideas he
entertained formed a strange medley of the rational
and irrational. He understood that all around
him were ill, but, at the same time, saw in each of
them some disguised character whom he had
known before, or of whom he had read and heard.
The asylum, he thought, was filled with men of
all times and countries,—the living and the dead.
Among them were famous and strong men of the
world, and not a few of the soldiers who had been

killed in the last war, but had risen from their
graves. He imagined he was in a kind of magic
circle that included the entire strength of the
world, and in proud rapture he counted himself to
be the centre of that circle. He and they, his
companions in the asylum, were all there for the
purpose of fulfilling a task, that vaguely presented
itself to his mind as a gigantic work, directed towards the destruction of evil on the earth. He
did not know how that task would be effected,
but felt within him strength sufficient to accomplish it." Or, what can be more true than the
picture he draws of the short intervals he enjoyed
of undisturbed reason, quickly followed by relapses
into stark madness. "He awoke in the night.
All was quiet; from the neighbouring large room
could be heard the heavy breathing of the
slumbering patients. Somewhere, in the distance,
a madman, who had been lodged for the night
in a dark chamber, was talking to himself in a
strained monotonous tone; and above, in one of
the rooms in the women's division, a hoarse-voiced
contralto was singing a wild uproarious song. The
sick man listened to these sounds. He felt a
strange weakness and languor in all his limbs, and
his neck ached violently. Where am I? What
has happened to me! were the questions that

flitted through his mind.   And suddenly, with
unusual clearness, all that had happened in the
last month came back to him, and he knew he
was ill, and he knew what his illness was.   He
recalled all the foolish thoughts, words, and acts,
and, at the remembrance, his whole body shook
and was convulsed.   But all that is over now,
thank God! Of course, it is all over! he murmured,
and again fell asleep.   And when he awoke, for
some minutes he possessed his full reason and was
seemingly quite well, only to get up from his bed
as mad as he had been before."

There are two points admirably brought out in
this unique and strangely interesting study of a
diseased mind.   In the moments when reason
returns to the hero, he invariably feels a dull
bodily weakness come over him, but the instant
he experiences the first slight excitement of madness, this weakness disappears and is replaced by
an   extravagant   energy,   and   an   uncontrollable
activity, that causes him to march about his room
with   hurried, uneven steps, talking and gesticu-
lating   all   the   while,   and   frequently   stumbling
against whatever may be in his way, and from the
shock receiving heavy blows that do not seem to
hurt or pain, and to which he pays no attention.
Further,   there   is   in   his   maddest   wanderings

and fancies an association of ideas as marked as
any sequence of thought in a healthy brain. "He
did not sleep all that night. He had plucked the
flower, because in that act he recognised the work
of his life, the task allotted to him by fate. The very
first time he happened to glance through the window of his room, its red leaflets had attracted his
attention, and now he felt that he had been faithful
to his call, and had done the work to accomplish
which life had been granted him. In its bright
red colour was concentrated all the evil of the
world. Of course, he knew that opium was
produced from the poppy, and it may be this
knowledge took a fantastic shape and suggested to
him the queer fancy that ere long completely
possessed his mind. In his eyes, the flower realised
in itself all existing evil; it had drunk in all the
innocent blood that had ever been poured forth,
and that is why it was so red, all the tears that
had ever been shed by the victims of human rage
and spleen. It was the personification of the
proud, cruel Ahriman, the enemy to God, who
had assumed this humble and seemingly innocent
form. It was his call to pluck and destroy it.
But that was not all. It must not be allowed,
while fading away, to diffuse its poisoned breath
abroad. For this reason he hid it in his bosom

o

He hoped that by the morning the flower would have lost all its strength. Its poison would penetrate into his breast, his very soul, and there be conquered or conquer; and if it conquered, he must perish and die,—but he would then die like a brave fighter, the first true champion of mankind, since no one before him had dared to try and crush at one blow all the evil of this world." There are other details in the story that deserve to be noticed, but I must content myself with selecting one. In the final scene,—the only part of the tale that is fictitious and invented,—the crazed hero is found dead on his couch: "and on his face lay the seal of unruffled peace and repose, and his worn features bore an expression of proud happiness and contentment." The artistic beauty of the scene must be evident to all, but it is also characterised by a scientific truthfulness that we do not always find in works of fiction. As the best pathologists have remarked, the higher qualities of a man are not destroyed, though they may from time to time be weakened and transformed by mental maladies; and thus the noble unselfishness of the hero of our story, and his capacity to devote himself to what he believes to be the cause of humanity, remain to the last fresh and vivid, and give him strength to die peacefully and gladly.

Simplicity, which, I need scarcely say, by no
means implies banality of style or poverty of in-
vention, has been, from the days of Poushkin, the
crowning characteristic of Russian poetry and
fiction.   Unfortunately, not a few later writers,
tempted by the prevailing taste for realistic sen-
sationalism, have adopted the tone and manner-
isms of a foreign school of novelists.   It is for
this reason we are justified in placing such a high
value on the works of those who have not fallen in
with a passing fashion, but have persistently
remained faithful to the better traditions of
Russian literature.   Of all our contemporary
novelists, M. Garschine and M. Korolenko have
the most closely followed in the steps of the great
Russian writers, and their works are the produc-
tions of true poets who have no need to resort to
the petty artifices of an affected and pretentious
style in order to win the interest of their readers.
There is a rare beauty in M. Korolenko's description of forest scenery that reminds us of
Tourgenieff, and it is impossible not to be struck
with the reserved power and delicacy of touch
with which these pictures are filled up.   The life,
the sounds, the colours of the forest, are well
known to him ; he is familiar with the varying
phases of its growth ; the murmuring leaves of the

oak, the elm, the fir, and the beech, have for him their distinct and peculiar melody ; and the stir and the movement of each tree are reproduced without effort. " In the forest there was always a murmur, regular, continuous, like the faint echo of a distant peal of bells ; soft and indistinct, like a song without words, or like the confused recollection of bygone days. The murmur never ceased by day or night, for it was an old dense forest of pines that had never been touched by woodman's saw or axe. Lofty pines, a hundred years old, with their red, sturdy trunks, stood in close array, waving, in response to each breath of wind, their high-tufted tops. Below, all was quiet ; the air was filled with an odour of tar ; through the thick layer of pine-cones, with which the ground was strewn, pushed gay ferns, in all the luxury of their rich fringes, and standing motionless, their leaves unstirred by the breeze. In damp nooks green grasses rose up on their high stalks ; and the white clover bent its heavy head, overcome, as it were, with dreamy lassitude. And above flowed the murmur of the forest, the mingling sighs of the old pine-wood."

The title-page of M. Korolenko's " Blind Musician" informs us that it is "a psychological study." The same may be said of all his tales.

The inner life of man is his favourite theme. He penetrates to the soul of man ; seeks out the moving principle of acts which seem to be the mere impulses of an ill-regulated nature ; and is thus able to present, in one harmonious whole, the complex workings of the human machine. His personages are, therefore, by reason of the varied, at times contradictory, elements of which they are composed, living creatures, and not, as with so many novelists, personifications of a pre-conceived idea. Take, for example, Vasielie, the hero of "The Sakhalientzie." He is naturally endowed with a restless, unsubdued energy : the monotony of home soon becomes insupportable, notwithstanding the ease and comfort with which his youth is surrounded ; and the mild Siberian steppes tempt him to commence a wandering vagabond life. He tells the story of his escape from the island of Sakhalin, and the listeners are stirred with an unrest similar to that which had led Vasielie himself to throw up all and risk the dangers and shame of a law-breaking career. This, however, is but the impression produced at first, and, in spite of the cool, daring tone he assumes, we before long come to know him better than, perhaps, he would care to have us know him. His passionate love of adventure, the indifference to human suffering and contempt for moral right, which were the fruits of his inordinate desire to live freely, had only touched the surface of the man's nature, and his better instincts, which he had schooled himself to crush,—love for his country and home, and a yearning for the life he professed to despise,—have, in reality, preserved their full force. "'Are you content with your life?' I asked, glancing up at the vagrant. He smiled, but his face wore a puzzled look. 'Life?' he said, and then paused, as he threw a fresh log of wood on to the fire. The flames lighted up his features, but his bright eyes had lost their wonted brilliancy. 'Eh, sir, if I were to relate to you . . . Then I saw nothing good in life, nor do I see any good now. Till I was eighteen I knew what is good in life, and I lived well and happily so long as I obeyed and listened to my parents. And when I refused to do so any longer life was over for me. From that day I reckon I ceased to live. It is so, and it is no use pretending it is not.' And, as he spoke, his face became darkened, and his lower lip trembled nervously, like a young child's, as if in this moment he had returned to the age when he 'listened to his parents,' as if once more he was a child, but the child was now ready to weep over the life he had wilfully cast away."

As we might expect, the subject of his story, "The Blind Musician," affords M. Korolenko abundant material for the exercise of his peculiar talent. The mental history of the boy, surrounded from his birth by an ever-during dark, the persistent struggle of his fancy to break. down the bar that shut to him the book of nature ; the feverish development of a keen quickness of hearing, as if to recompense him for the deprivation of sight; all this is described with rare picturesqueness and poetic truthfulness. "The boy figured to himself depth in the form of the soft murmur of the stream as it flowed at the foot of the precipice, or of the frightened splash of pebbles thrown from its top. Distance sounded in his ears like the confused notes of a dying song. At times, in the sultry noonday, when over the whole of nature there reigns a quiet so profound that we can only divine the uninterrupted noiseless course of life, the face of the blind boy would light up with a strange expression. It seemed as if, under the influence of the silence that prevailed around, there rose up from the depth of his soul sounds audible only to himself, and to which he was listening with rapt attention. It was easy to believe that at such moments a vague, but productive, train of thought was awakening in his soul, like to the imperfectly

caught melody of an unknown song." Naturally
of a lively and active disposition, as the months
went by, blindness set its mark upon its character,
and whilst still a child he lost much of his gaiety,
and liked to sit for hours in the corner of his room,
with the quiet, hushed air of one who is listening ;
and if by chance any one entered, an expression of
annoyance would come over his face, as though
the noise of the opening door had broken the
charm of the world of sound wherein he lived, and
with which he loved to commune. The outer
world was known to him only through sound, and
as he grew up, with each year he found fresh and
wider means of receiving those impressions which
others obtain by sight.

There is a fascinating originality in M. Korolenko's tale, entitled, " A Dream of After-Death."
Its hero, Macarius, lived at Chalgan, an obscure
Siberian village, in the far-off marshes of Yakut ;
" where he worked hard, lived poorly, and endured
hunger and cold." But dull and irksome as his
life was, Macarius, like other men, had his visions
of a happier possible future, and particularly when
he was drunk would indulge in vague dreams of
throwing up his home and setting forth in search
of the blessed country that lay beyond the mountains, and of which he had often heard the elders

of the Yakut village tell such wonderful stories. " What kind of mountains they were, or where they were to be found, he did not exactly know ; all he knew was, that there were such mountains, and that they were far, far, away ;—so far, that no police-sergeant could ever get at him. There he would not have to plough, or sow, or fell trees, or bring in timber, or grind corn with a hand mill-stone. There he would have nothing to do, except to pray and earn his salvation. And, of course, he would no longer have to pay Government taxes." On the day when we first make his acquaintance, poor Macarius is perfectly sober, and as is always the case with him under such circumstances, in a sad and melancholy mood. "It was Christmas Eve, and Macarius knew that to-morrow was a great holiday. For that reason he wished to celebrate the day like a good Christian, and to lay in some drink ; but unfortunately he had no means to buy any. He had long ago disposed of all his corn, and was already in debt to every shopkeeper and Tartar of the place. What kind of life was that, when even on the great winter feast a man could not have his bottle of brandy ?" With some difficulty he, however, succeeds in disposing of five loads of wood, which he promises to supply on a fixed date, and receives a rouble in advance, with which, of course, he at once hurries off to the nearest Tartar inn. On his way home he surprises a certain Alexis, poaching on his grounds, and in his pursuit of the marauder gets lost in the forest, and after long and vain efforts to find the path, sinks down to die in the snow. " How he died, and in what death consisted, he did not exactly remark. He knew that something ought to go out of him, and waited for it to do so. But nothing went out of him. Still he was conscious that he had died, and lay quiet, without moving. He lay for a long time,—indeed, so long that at last he got tired of it. It was quite dark when Macarius felt some one give him a gentle kick. He turned his head and opened his shut eyes. The bare boughs of the larch trees were spread peacefully over him ; the shaggy fir-trees waved gently their snow-covered branches ; the flakes of snow hovered softly in the clear fresh air ; and the bright pure stars peered down from the blue sky into the dense forest, and whispered to one another : ' See, a poor man has died.' It was the old priest, Ivan, who stood over the body of Macarius, pushing it gently with his foot. His long cassock was covered with snow, and snow had fallen on his fur cap, his shoulders, and his long beard. But what was most strange of all, this same priest, Ivan, had died four years

ago." The priest tells Macarius that he must get
up and go with him to the great Lord Toyon ; and
though poor Macarius thinks " it is a shame that
even after death a man cannot be left in peace,"
there is nothing to be done, and he grumblingly
obeys. It was a long and difficult journey they
made together, nor was the poor peasant at all
pleased with the conditions under which he had
to tramp on, as he followed his guide along the
seemingly endless straight road that led them
towards the east. " 'Have we much farther to
go ?' asked Macarius. 'A long way yet,' shortly
answered the priest. 'And where can we get
something to eat ?' anxiously demanded Macarius.
'You forget,' answered the priest, turning round,
' you are dead, and do not want anything to eat or
to drink.' Macarius was not very pleased with
this reply. Of course, it was no good grumbling
if there really was nothing to eat, but then they
should have let him lie still and quiet after death.
But to have to walk, and to walk for miles too,
without anything to eat, struck him as being
quite contrary to the natural order of things.
And again he began to grumble. 'Do not grumble !' said the priest. 'All right,' he muttered
in a surly tone, but continued to growl to
himself at his hard fate. Who ever heard of

making a man walk and walk, and all the while refuse to give him a bit of something to eat? And so, they continue to march on and on for a number of days, till at last they find themselves before a large beautiful hut, and with the words, 'Let us enter, we have arrived at the end of our journey,' the good priest leads him in. Some servants of the great Toyon make inquiries of the priest as to who it is he has brought with him, and then conduct them to the middle of the hut, where stood a pair of huge scales, and bid them wait till Toyon appears. Macarius asked the priest what the scales were wanted for, and why they were so large. 'You see,' replied the priest, a little confused, 'the scales are required to weigh the good and evil each one of us has done during his lifetime. With most the good and evil are pretty equally balanced; but the Chalganians are such sinners that Toyon ordered special scales to be made for them, and the bowl in which their sins are weighed is enormously large.' Macarius felt rather uncomfortable on hearing this, and began to be frightened. He remarked that one of the bowls was of pure gold and very diminutive in size; the other was of wood and of huge proportions. Under the latter a deep black hole suddenly opened in the ground. Macarius went up and examined the scales, to see if there was nothing wrong about them. But they were strictly accurate and stood perfectly balanced. For this very reason he did not quite understand their construction, the more so as all his life he had had to do with scales that invariably enabled him to sell and buy with advantage and profit to himself. And whilst he is thus wondering the aged Toyon enters. Macarius is asked who he was, his name and age, whence he came, and what he had done in his lifetime. In his reply to these searching questions the peasant who, strange to say, remembers each stroke of his axe, each tree he had felled, each furrow he had made, and each field he had ploughed, takes care to add a few thousand trees and fathoms of wood, in the hope of exciting the aged Toyon's sympathy and pity. But, to his fright, Toyon sends the priest to fetch a large book, in which is entered every detail of the whole life of Macarius, and orders him to read out all his sins that from day to day had been re-corded against him. And whilst he read the white-winged servants put into the golden scale the timber and trees he had cut down, and all the field-work he had done. And the sum total amounted to so much that the golden scale rose up high beyond the reach of man; and the young angels flew to the top beam and with ropes pulled it down. The life of the poor Chalganian had been hard and toilsome! After this, priest Ivan began to read out the cheats of which he had been guilty, and it appeared they were twenty-one thousand nine hundred and thirty-three in number; and next he read how many bottles of brandy he had drunk, and they were four hundred in all; and the priest read on, and poor Macarius saw the wooden scale drag down the golden one, and each moment it sank lower into the hole dug beneath it; and still the priest went on reading, and still the scale continued to fall." Sentence is pronounced, and Macarius is condemned to serve as beast of burden to the police-sergeant and the church-manciple of Chaligan, who are well known to carry the heaviest of loads and to drive their horses at fullest speed. At the same time he is asked if he can allege any just cause why the sentence should not be carried into execution. And then the strangest of things happens. Macarius, who had never been able to put together ten words consecutively, suddenly feels within him the gift of speech, and pleads for justice with a power and persuasiveness the most practised of orators might have envied.

" He began by saying that he did not wish to serve as horse to the church-manciple. And if he did not wish, it was not because he feared hard work, but because the sentence was an unjust one. And since it was an unjust one, he would never submit to it. Let them do what they liked with him, he would never budge a step! Let them give him to the devil, to be tormented for all eternity, he would never carry the police-sergeant, because it was unjust! And do not let them suppose that he was too proud to take the place of a horse! The manciple drives his horse far and sharply, but he at least finds him good oats; and he had been driven and hunted about all his life, and no one had ever fed him with oats or with anything else. . . . . Yes, they had driven and hunted him all his life! The village mayor and his officials, the police-sergeants and their underlings had hunted him to force taxes out of him; the priests, with their church dues, had hunted him; poverty and hunger had hunted him; cold and heat had hunted him; rain and drought had hunted him; the frozen ground and evil forest had hunted him. The beasts of the field are driven on, and they hang down their heads to the ground, and know not whither they are driven! And so it had been with him. Did he, then, know what it was the priest read in church, or why he took his fees and dues? Did he, then, know why, or whither, they carried off his eldest son, when they made him a soldier, or where he died, and where his bleached bones are lying? . . . They say he added on three thousand trees. And suppose he did. If he cut down only sixteen thousand,—is that so little? Besides, two thousand of these trees he cut down when his first wife was ill. And his heart was heavy, and he longed to sit by the old woman, but want and poverty drove him to the woods. And there, in the forest, he wept, and the tears froze on his eyelids, and sorrow and cold pierced to his very heart. But for all that he set to work, and cut down the trees. And then his old wife died, and he must bury her, but he had no money. He got some work in the woods, so that he might earn money enough to pay for the old woman's lodging in the next world. The wood-merchant saw he was hard up, and gave him ten copecks apiece. And the old woman was all the while lying cold and alone in the unwarmed hut, and he went into the forest to cut down the trees, and to weep. . . . They say that all his whole life is written down in that book. Will they try and find in it when he once received from any of his fellow-creatures a kindly word, an affectionate caress, or a good service? Where are his children, or what joy have they been to him? If they died, it was hard and bitter to him. If they lived and grew up, they went away, and left him to fight alone with want and hunger. And he had suffered alone with his second old woman, and had seen how little by little his strength forsook him, and evil, homeless, old age came upon him. They stood alone, like two orphaned fir-trees in the wide forest, scathed and beaten on every side by the cruel storm-wind."

The words of Macarius are not without effect. The aged Toyon is touched, and bids him "have patience, poor soul, thou art no longer on earth: here will be found justice, even for thee!" And as he spoke, the scales began to tremble, and the wooden bowl began to rise ever higher and higher.

THE END.

P

www.ingramcontent.com/pod-product-compliance
Lightning Source LLC
Chambersburg PA
CBHW020616030726
47497CB00007B/2274